LEARN A LOT ON THE POT

AMAZING FACTS AND TRIVIA ABOUT SCIENCE, HISTORY, ANIMALS, AND BEYOND THAT WILL BLOW YOUR MIND

SAM CALLISTER

© Copyright 2024 – Sam Callister – All rights reserved

The content within this book may not be reproduced, duplicated, or transmitted without direct written permission from the author or the publisher.

Under no circumstances will any blame or legal responsibility be held against the publisher, or author, for any damages, reparation, or monetary loss due to the information contained within this book, either directly or indirectly.

Legal Notice

This book is copyright protected. This book is only for personal use. You cannot amend, distribute, sell, use, quote, or paraphrase any part, or the content within this book, without the consent of the author-publisher.

Disclaimer Notice

Please note that the information contained within this document is for educational and entertainment purposes only. All effort has been executed to present accurate, up-to-date, and reliable, complete information. No warranties of any kind are declared or implied. Readers acknowledge that the author is not engaging in the rendering of legal, financial, medical, or professional advice.

Table of Content

Introduction 18

Chapter 1: Everyday Science in Your Bathroom 20

The Door and the Invisible Microbe Dance 20

Toilet Paper and Its Scientific Side 20

Myths Down the Drain 20

The Shimmering Illusion of Toothpaste 21

Foggy Mirrors and Mischievous Steam 21

The Hidden Ballet of Faucet Water 21

The Unsung Hero of Your Smile 22

Soap and Its Friendly Chemistry 22

The Tiny Zoo Under Your Sink 22

The Aroma Alchemy 23

The Hidden Crystals in Your Towel 23

Mold's Hidden Playground 23

Colorful Toilets and Ceramic Mastery 23

The Magic of Touchless Faucets 24

Behind the Scenes of a Smart Flush 24

Nature's Anti-Skid Trick 24

The Secret Grip of Anti-Slip Slippers 25

The Showerhead's Secret Artistry 25

The Hidden Shield of Your Shower Curtain 25

Moistened Toilet Paper 25

Chapter 2: History & Curiosities from the Past 27

Hygiene in Ancient Egypt 27

Absurd Victorian Inventions 27

The Bathing Rituals of Roman Emperors 27

Writing Tools Lost Over Time...28

Tales of Spies and Invisible Inks...28

Vanished Calendars and Quirky Timekeeping.............................28

When Barbers Were Surgeons 29

Medieval Maps with Imaginary Sea Monsters 29

Hidden Sanctuaries Beneath Ancient Pyramids 29

Oral Hygiene in the Time of Pharaohs......................................30

Banknotes, Shells, and Rock Salt...30

The Water Clock 30

The Mystery of Undeciphered Manuscripts 31

Secret Festivities in Forgotten Courts 31

The First Modern Toilet in History 31

Strange Duels and Improbable Weapons....................................32

Foods Reserved for Kings 32

The Origin of Surnames and Vanished Professions......................32

Love Letters on Tree Leaves 33

Exotic and Incomprehensible Funeral Ceremonies......................33

Chapter 3: Languages, Words & Communication 34

Untranslatable Words from Every Continent................................34

Proverbs with Ridiculous Origins 34

Lost Punctuation Marks..34

Alphabets Vanished Over the Centuries 35

Worlds Forged by Words 35

Medieval Ciphers and Secret Messages 36

The Funny Origin of Some Place Names.....................................36

Alphabetic Acrobatics 36

Dying Dialects Every Two Weeks...37

Borrowed Words from Other Languages 37

The Secret Language of Market Vendors 37

When Sound Changes Meaning 38

Whistled Languages and Remote Tribes 38

The Global Journey of "Ciao" 38

Hand Gestures with Different Meanings Everywhere 38

The Longest Word in a Dictionary 39

Mysterious Signs and Symbols Carved in Stone 39

Military Codes That Remain Unbroken 39

The Language of Flowers: Silent Messages in Blooms 40

Onomatopoeia Changing Across Cultures 40

Chapter 4: Nature, Animals & Extraordinary Plants 41

Animals That Glow in the Dark 41

Carnivorous Plants Beyond Imagination 41

Insect Architects: Astonishing Nests and Hives 41

Flowers That Smell Like Corpses 42

Birds That Mimic Cellphone Ringtones 42

Fish That Walk on Land 42

Mammals That Lay Eggs 43

Giant Underground Fungi 43

Monkeys Stealing Your Sunglasses 43

The Chameleon's Secret 44

The World's Oldest Trees 44

Forests That Communicate Underground 44

Marine Creatures That Don't Age 45

Deserts in Bloom 45

Rodents as Shiny Collectors 45

The Wolf's Howl 45

Bacteria Thriving in Volcanoes 46

Butterflies Migrating with Incredible Routes 46

Pink Lakes and Rainbow Oceans 46

Dancing Bees: Choreographies of Coordinates 47

Chapter 5: Food Cooking and Curious Eating Habits 48

Honey That Never Dies..48

Fruits From a World of Wonders 48

Fermentations That Challenge Taste and Courage 48

Ancient Tea Rituals That Amaze 49

Cacao Seeds Once Worth a Fortune...49

Insects on the Table a New Culinary Frontier...49

Medieval Recipes a Bizarre Feast..50

Foods That Change Flavor When Observed..50

Sushi a Legend Reinvented Through Time 50

Camel Milk and Unexpected Dairy Discoveries 51

Sparkling Drinks Born From Flowers 51

Record Hot Peppers a Flame to Challenge...51

Sacred Foods and Rituals by the Fire..52

Pasta and Pizza Myths to Debunk..52

Space Cuisine Beyond Tubes and Purées 52

Savory Smoothies and Surprising Blends 52

Glutamate the Truth Behind the Myth..53

The Potato a History Rich in Mysteries 53

Gelatinized Foods and Curious Past Trends 53

Ancestral Broths With a Hint of Magic 54

Chapter 6: Arts and Entertainment 55

Paintings Made With Unexpected Pigments...55

Musical Instruments Built From Scrap..55

Sand Sculptures That Challenge Time 55

Silent Cinema Hiding Secret Sounds Behind the Scenes 56

Art Installations Drifting on Icebergs 56

Modern Puppeteers Weaving Ancient Tales 56

Photography Without a Camera..57

Hidden Theaters in Unimaginable Places 57

Murals That Come Alive With Optical Illusions..................................57

Bizarre Comics From Distant Cultures 58

Performances Where the Audience Becomes the Star 58

Artists Who Paint Using Unusual Body Parts 58

The Oldest Graffiti Made by Humankind..59

Rare Vinyl Records and Extreme Collectors 59

Films Shot Within a Single Room 59

Marionettes Dancing on Water...60

Endless Concerts That Break Records 60

Poems Written Backward to Puzzle the Mind.....................................60

Theatrical Costumes Stitched From Recycled Materials 61

Unusual Museums Devoted to the Strangest Things 61

Chapter 7: Sports Games and Astonishing Records 62

Soccer on Ice and the Art of Elegant Falling 62

Marathons in Costume a Parade of Smiling Runners 62

Underwater Chess Strategies in Apnea 63

Hula Hoop Marathons and the Triumph of Perseverance 63

Cars and a Ball the Absurd Motorized Match......................................63

Candy Cane Fencing a Sweet Duel 64

Tree Climbing the Evolution of a Childhood Game............................64

Pillow Fights for World Records Softest Showdown Ever..................64

Global Treasure Hunts and International Quests 65

Racing the Frozen Frontier..65

Sack Races Upgraded to Top-Level Competition 66

Bicycle on a Tightrope Nerves of Steel in Midair 66

Cellphone Tossing Liberation Through a Throw.................................66

Typing Wizards a Tribute to Speed and Precision..............................66

Living Chess Pieces and Theatrical Showdowns 67

Running Backward the World in Reverse 67

Beds on Wheels Racing Through Town 67

Dancing on Cooled Lava Testing the Extreme 68

Chapter 8: Mind Illusions and Psychological Curiosities 69

The Schrödinger's cat paradox and multiple perceptions in our minds 69

An Aroma That Unlocks Ancient Memories 69

The Glitch in Our Mental Timeline 69

The Trickery Behind Your Eyes 70

The Mind's Quest for Patterns 70

Colors and Flavors 70

When Senses Collide 71

The Contagious Power of a Smile 71

Music That Shapes Our Sense of Time 71

Order in Our Surroundings and Mood Changes 71

The Placebo Effect 72

Strange Phobias 72

Cognitive Biases 72

Finding Faces Everywhere 73

False Memories 73

Brilliant Ideas Under the Shower 73

Color Coding and Traffic Signs 73

Lucid Dreams 74

The Brain Filling in What's Not There 74

The Universe in a Blot 74

Chapter 9: Travels Traditions and Unusual Geographies 75

Tiny Nations, Big Stories 75

A Desert That Turns Into a Colorful Garden of Flowers 75

The Wandering Islands 75

Sunken Cities, Living Memories 76

Borders of Identity 76

Love's Quirky Traditions 76

Tea Rituals Beyond Expectations 76

Villages Where the Official Language Doesn't Exist......................77

Lanterns of Light and Hope 77

Sports and Dances of Remote Islands...78

Sacred Places Off-Limits to Most 78

Inverted Maps..78

Rainbow Mountains..78

Cities with Unusual Urban Geometry 79

Forgotten Pilgrimage Routes Through Silent Forests 79

The Bridge Linking Two Continents 79

Harvest Festivals with Eerie Masks 79

Floating Markets and Amphibious Cultures 80

Calendars That Don't Recognize 365 Days................................... 80

Chapter 10: Technology Gadgets and Bizarre Inventions..................... 81

The First Wearable Computer... 81

Robotic Chefs.. 81

Gadgets for Ironing Clothes on the Go... 81

Typewriters Sending Emails 82

A 3D-Printed Spare Wheel on Demand 82

Elevators Without Cables..82

Cars Changing Color at the Push of a Button 83

Devices That Translate Thoughts into Text....................................83

Houses Built in a Day..83

A Pen That Draws in Mid-Air..83

Objects That Repair Themselves..84

DNA-Based Computers..84

Tuning the Atmosphere to Your Mood 84

Holographic Films 84

Transparent Solar Panels 85

Anti-Gravity Backpacks 85

Shoes with Integrated GPS 85

Glasses That Brew Coffee? 85

A Singing Fridge 85

Share Your Experience 87

Chapter 11: Myths, Folklore & Imaginary Creatures 88

The Dragon Slumbering Beneath Ancient Mountains 88

Mischievous Woodland Fairies in the Northern Forests.....................88

Feathered Serpents of Mesoamerica...88

The Celtic Water Horse...89

The American Mothman..89

Ghostly Lights in Desert Nights...89

The Latin American Chupacabra 90

The Golem's Eternal Lesson 90

Marine Demons and Krakens in Northern Sagas..............................90

The Deer-Woman 91

Lamassu of Mesopotami...91

Sirens and the Irresistible Call of Ruin 91

Werewolves and the Beast Within Man 91

Vampires Beyond Europe 92

Talking Trees in African Lore 92

Lake Monsters 92

The Himalayan Yeti 92

Mischievous Teachers of Hidden Truths 93

The Evolution of the Mythical Unicorn...93

The Phoenix and the Promise of Rebirth from Fire 93

Chapter 12: Pop Culture & Absurd Trends 94

Viral Fads Born Out of Nowhere 94

Popular Dances on Social Media 94

Collectible Gadgets Inspired by TV Shows 94

Music Festivals in the Most Unlikely Places 95

Carnival Costumes Inspired by Memes 95

Food Branded by Pop Stars and Influencers 95

Why Redo Everything? 96

Pop Stars Without Bodies 96

Odd Museums Devoted to Celebrities 96

Themed Restaurants Paying Homage to Cult Films 96

Movie Props Sold at Absurd Prices 97

Cartoons Turned into Fashion Legends 97

Secret Cameos by Directors in Their Films 97

Musical Covers in Invented Languages 97

Karaoke Fever Taken to the Extreme 98

Vintage Objects Cycling Back into Style 98

Internet Slang That Vanishes in a Blink 98

The World's Strangest Fan Clubs 99

Online Fandom Wars 99

TV Marathons of Old Forgotten Series 99

Chapter 13: Extraordinary Science 100

Bacteria Discovered by Chance on a Forgotten Sandwich ...100

Discoveries Born from Flawed Experiments 100

The Creature That Survives in Open Space 100

Secret Labs Beneath Polar Ice 101

Brains Preserved to Understand the Human Mind 101

Monkeys Learning to Use Tablets 101

Plants That 'Make Music'—Or Something Like It? 102

Biological Cryptographers 102

Particles That Appear and Vanish into Nothing 102

The Mystery of Dark Matter 102

Fossils of Bizarre Creatures Never Seen Before 103

Sleep Experiments Uncovering Nightmares 103

Metals That Melt in Your Hand 103

A Robot That Learns Like a Child 104

Mini-Brains Grown in Test Tubes 104

Genetic Engineering and 'Spider Goats' 104

Microbes That Feast on Plastic 104

Artificial Volcanoes in the Lab 105

Giant Telescopes in Underground Caves 105

Physics Labs on Space Stations.. 105

Chapter 14: Literature, Authors & Unusual Books 106

Famous Novelists with Secret Pen Names 106

Encrypted Manuscripts Never Deciphered 106

Floating Libraries on Ships 106

Books Forbidden and Burned Through the Ages 107

Poetry Written on Leaves and Bark 107

Authors Who Hated Their Most Famous Works............................... 107

Novels Generated by Algorithms 108

Stories Transmitted Only Orally 108

The World's Strangest Bookstores... 108

Biographies of Imaginary Animals 109

Inks Made from Improbable Substances 109

Stories Illustrated by Child Prodigies 109

Books Without Vowels... 109

Interactive Stories with Multiple Endings 110

Authors Who Wrote Only at Night..110

Novels Printed on Recycled Old Newspapers.. 110

Anthologies of Nonsense Phrases 111

Love Letters Between Rival Authors 111

Unique Copies of Books Lost Forever 111

The Shortest Novel and the Longest Story 111

Chapter 15: Wonders of the Body & Curious Wellness Tips.................113

Medicinal Plants Grown on Rooftops 113

Massages Performed with Ice Stones...113

Intermittent Fasting in Ancient Times..113

Grandma's Remedies for Toothache..114

Desert Saunas 114

Yoga Suspended in Midair 114

Thermal Treatments with Volcanic Mud 115

Massages with Snakes,...115

Acupuncture with Fish Spines?...115

Breathing Techniques Against Stress..116

Therapeutic Forests 116

Unusual Hiccup Cures 116

Cleopatra's Donkey Milk Baths in Antiquity 117

Swing-Based Workouts for Balance 117

Little-Known Anti-Stress Foods..117

Curing Insomnia with Whale Sounds 117

Scalp Massages with Bone Combs...118

Ritual Fasting and Effects on the Mind..118

Aromatic Essences as Natural 'Vaccines' 118

Eye Exercises for Hawk-Like Vision 119

Chapter 16: Debunking Myths & Urban Legends 120

A Glass of Water on the TV 120

Does Chewing Gum Stay in Your Stomach for Years?................................120

Is the Sea Really Trapped in a Seashell's Sound?............................120

Frogs Raining from the Sky 121

Is the Toilet Seat the Dirtiest Place? 121

Do Goldfish Really Have a Memory of Mere Seconds? 121

Does Sugar Make Children Hyperactive? 121

Does Cutting Your Hair Make It Grow Back Stronger?....................122

Do Lightning Bolts Never Strike the Same Place Twice? 122

Do Ostriches Bury Their Heads in the Sand? 122

Do Hair Turn White Suddenly After a Shock? 122

Were the Pyramids Built by Aliens?..123

Is Eating Before Swimming Dangerous? 123

Miracle Mud Packs to Instantly Lose Fat? 123

Do Vaccines Cause Absurd Diseases? 124

Is There a Safe Time to Stare at the Sun? 124

Hairdryer in the Bathtub: Just a Myth? 124

Sleeping with Plants in the Room is Dangerous?.............................124

Spinach as an Extraordinary Source of Iron 124

The Great Wall Visible from Space?..125

Chapter 17: Outdoor Oddities & Survival Secrets 126

Plants That Thrive in the Impossible 126

Finding Your Way Without Compass or GPS....................................126

How Animals Survive in Harsh Conditions 126

Crazy Climates and Incredible Survival Stories 127

Edible Wild Foods You Never Considered 127

Filtering Water with Your T-Shirt...127

Communicating at a Distance with Smoke Signals 128

Frogs Frozen and Revived 128

Tree Resin as Natural Glue 128

Fishing with Rudimentary Traps 129

Cooking Over Fire Without Pots 129

Nutrient-Rich Insects in the Forest... 129

Testing a Berry for Poison.. 130

Interpreting Animal Tracks 130

Recognizing Local Medicinal Plants... 130

Making Rope from Plant Fibers 131

Preserving Food Without a Fridge 131

Purifying Water by Boiling Stones 131

Predicting Weather by Watching Clouds 132

Facing a Bear Encounter... 132

Chapter 18: Curiosities about Riddles, Puzzles & Brain-Teasers 133

The Riddle of the Sphinx... 133

Kakuro, Sudoku's Lesser-Known Cousin 133

Simple Ciphers for Beginners 133

Medieval Riddles on Parchment 134

Tangram Puzzles and Impossible Figures 134

Ancient Mazes Recreated in Gardens... 134

Magic Squares and Lucky Numbers 135

Rebus Puzzles Merging Images and Words 135

Mental Mind Games 135

Gordian Knots... 135

The Barber Paradox 136

Rubik's Cubes with Impossible Shapes 136

Rhymed Riddles in Popular Tradition 136

Interlocking Rings 137

3D Chess Variants... 137

The Coin-Weighing Puzzle.. 137

Matchstick Puzzles and Everyday Ingenuity 137

Venn Diagrams and Improbable Deductions 138

The Königsberg Bridges Enigma.. 138

Discoveries About Paper Puzzles and Ingenious Origami................................ 138

Chapter 19: Time, the Future & Temporal Oddities 139

Alternative Calendars Used in Isolated Communities 139

Prophets Who Foresaw Modern Inventions 139

Ancient Literature's Idea of Time Travel 139

The Internet Era Imagined a Century Ago 140

Old Clocks That Measured More Than Just Time............................ 140

Bizarre Time Zones in Small Nations 140

The Phenomenon of the 'Delayed' New Year 141

Time in Parallel Dimensions:...141

Past Predictions of Futures That Never Came True 141

Time Machines in Secret (or Nearly So) Museums............................141

Alternate Timelines in Comics... 142

Archeology of the Future: Imagining Tomorrow's Past 142

Endless Nights Near the Earth's Poles.. 142

Atomic Clocks and Incredible Precision 143

The 10-Day Week... 143

The Man Who Tried to Stop Time 143

Aztec Prophecies That Never Happened.. 143

Time Zones Invented for Political Reasons....................................... 144

Animal Perceptions of Time... 144

Interstellar Travel and Time Dilation 144

Chapter 20: The Great Mixture—Random Revelations 145

Coincidences Too Strange to Be Mere Chance..................................145

Weird Collections from Every Corner of the World 145

Letters Delivered Decades Late 145

Elevators That Move Diagonally... 146

People Living on Islands of Plastic Waste 146

World Records for the Longest Hair 146

Villages Where Everyone Shares the Same Surname 147

Contests for the World's Strangest Mustaches 147

Ghost Photos.. 147

Sculptures Made from Chewed Gum 148

Square Coins and Plastic Banknotes 148

Musical Roads That Sing as You Drive... 148

Artist Colonies Living Underground 149

Giant Pinhole Cameras 149

Bridges Made from Living Roots 149

Cryptocurrencies Born from Strange Memes.. 150

Houses Inside Abandoned Buses.. 150

Penguin Colonies in Unexpected Places.. 150

Underground Metropolises and Invisible Cities 150

People Spending Life in Hot-Air Balloons 151

Thanks for Making It This Far 152

Conclusion **153**

About the Author.. **155**

17

Introduction

Did you know there's a village where nearly everyone shares the same last name, forcing the local mail carrier to perform heroic feats just to tell one "John Smith" from another? Or that penguins can thrive in places far milder than the icy landscapes we imagine, shattering our classic mental picture? And what about living bridges woven from tree roots, growing sturdier over time as if nature herself were a patient and gifted engineer? These are just a few examples of the marvels you'll find in the pages ahead—a real market stall of curiosities, where every corner hides a surprising fact, a mind-boggling anecdote, or an unexpected discovery.

Imagine yourself in a quiet moment, alone, door closed, perhaps in the comfort of your bathroom's peaceful solitude. Instead of simply scrolling through social media, why not turn this brief pause into a mental adventure? That's where this book comes in: it transforms an ordinary break into a chance to explore the world from new angles. Flip to any page and you might stumble upon stories of square coins or joke-inspired cryptocurrencies. Turn another page and you'll find tales of "ghost" photographs debunked as tricks of light, or roads engineered to sing melodies beneath your car's tires.

Have you ever wondered why some remote communities don't follow our January-February-March pattern, basing their calendars instead on the blooming of certain flowers or the rhythm of the tides? Or how a letter can arrive decades late, turning a mundane note into a time-traveling whisper from the past? This book revels in these kinds of questions—strange truths spanning the globe and human history. It reminds us that reality often outdoes fantasy, and that objects, people, and places we dismiss as ordinary can hide a story, a record, or a peculiarity worth celebrating.

As you read, you'll encounter ancient clocks that measured more than hours, artists who sculpt with chewed gum, underground art colonies, diagonal elevators, penguin colonies thriving in unexpected climates, and festive chaos where New Year's might start on a day you'd never anticipate. Sometimes you'll find straightforward lists of oddities; other times, mini-stories about little-known historical episodes. Throughout it all, the tone remains lively and playful, like a friend pointing out one astonishing thing after another, nudging you to say, "Wow, who'd have thought?"

Each page invites you to rediscover the world with fresh eyes. Maybe after reading, you'll spot unusual details in your everyday surroundings. There's no linear storyline, no overarching lesson—just an eclectic collection of tidbits, drifting like treasures in a flea market of the extraordinary. Sometimes you'll smile, sometimes you'll be struck silent, sometimes you'll shake your head in disbelief.

Whether you have seconds or minutes, this book is your unpredictable companion, always ready with another surprising gem. The stage is yours: browse, marvel, and let curiosity take charge. You decide where to start, because here, wonder follows no set path. Enjoy!

Chapter 1:
Everyday Science in Your Bathroom

The Door and the Invisible Microbe Dance

Would you ever think that the bathroom door handle, that small piece of metal or plastic you touch absentmindedly, could host more bacteria than the toilet seat itself? Yet, laboratory tests have shown that certain handles can harbor thousands of microorganisms per square centimeter, including strains like Staphylococcus aureus. This surprising fact turns our assumptions upside down: everyone suspects the toilet, but the door handle is actually a hidden ballroom for tiny, invisible guests. Don't panic, though: washing your hands with plain soap and water drastically reduces this "microbe crowd." A common gesture, incredibly effective, making a real difference.

Toilet Paper and Its Scientific Side

It may seem trivial, but toilet paper is a small marvel of engineering. The cellulose fibers, obtained from wood, are processed and interlaced to form a sheet that's soft yet sturdy enough for the job at hand. When it comes into contact with the toilet's water, these fibers separate easily, preventing clogs. Some varieties are more eco-friendly, others focus on extra softness. Next time you tear off a piece, remember you're using a refined product, the result of industrial evolution and clever chemical insights. It's more ingenious than you'd think.

Myths Down the Drain

Ever heard the story that in the Southern Hemisphere the toilet water swirls in the opposite direction? It's just a myth. The vortex you see is determined by the toilet's internal shape, the position of the water jets, and your home's water pressure—not by the Coriolis effect. The

Coriolis force influences large-scale weather patterns, not the tiny waterscape in your bathroom. Pressing the flush unleashes a miniature, carefully designed whirlpool to whisk away waste. It's a simple engineering trick that turns an everyday act into a neat little water show, flushing away false beliefs with a quiet swirl.

The Shimmering Illusion of Toothpaste

Squeezing toothpaste onto your brush might look like creating a little party of light and color, but there's no neon magic at play. Instead, some particles in the paste reflect the bathroom's lighting. Toothpaste blends mild abrasives, fluoride, and flavorings to protect and clean your teeth, while the "sparkling" effect is merely a trick of reflections. No alien glow on your toothbrush—just a thoughtfully balanced formula for a healthy smile. Funny how behind that gleaming impression lies a simple combination of chemistry and good taste, all working for your dental well-being.

Foggy Mirrors and Mischievous Steam

After a hot shower, your mirror becomes a blank canvas, erasing your reflection. Blame the steam: warm water vapor hits the cooler surface of the mirror, turning into tiny droplets that scatter light, making everything look hazy. A simple household trick is to rub a thin layer of soap on the mirror, reducing the steam's grip. This way, you can spot your face right away, no waiting required. It's a small daily scene that unites physics and cleverness, granting you a few extra seconds of clear vision each morning.

The Hidden Ballet of Faucet Water

Turn on the faucet and see a steady ribbon of water. Behind this simplicity lies a world of pipes, water pressure, and gravity. Water flows because your home's plumbing pushes it with the right force, while the shape of the sink and surface tension create subtle eddies. A larger drain hole speeds the flow; a smaller one slows it down. Everything is in balance, allowing you to wash your hands so effortlessly. A commonplace act, orchestrated by physical forces harmonizing invisibly each time you reach for that stream.

The Unsung Hero of Your Smile

Sitting in a glass next to the sink is a modest hero: your toothbrush. Its bristles scrub away plaque and bacteria, protecting enamel and gums. Store it upright, uncovered, and replace it every two or three months—bent or tired bristles do less work. No futuristic gadget needed, just this quiet daily warrior at your service. Think of it as a bristle sword fighting invisible battles morning and night. A humble tool, yet essential for keeping your grin in top shape.

Soap and Its Friendly Chemistry

Soap is a mediator between water and dirt. Its molecules have one part that loves water and another that loves oils. When you lather up, these molecules "grab" grease and grime, trapping them in tiny bubbles that rinse away easily. A simple but brilliant process, perfected over centuries. Each time you create foam, you're staging a chemical dance that turns your hands into a neutral, clean territory. A daily ritual blending science and cleanliness in just a few seconds.

The Tiny Zoo Under Your Sink

The toilet and sink aren't barren spaces—they're tiny ecosystems filled with microorganisms. Some studies show that objects like smartphones or keyboards can be even "dirtier" than the toilet, shattering the myth that the bathroom is the ultimate microbial villain. Regular cleaning and handwashing keep everything in check. No need to live in fear: bacteria are part of life. It's intriguing that what we assume to be filthy isn't always worse than everyday gadgets. The moral? A bit of hygiene and common sense are enough to coexist peacefully with this unseen zoo.

The Aroma Alchemy

Air fresheners work by releasing tiny scent molecules. Some neutralize bad odors, others mask them with citrus or floral notes. There's no magic, just chemistry at play. Choose a pleasant fragrance and your bathroom transforms into a mini aromatic garden. Amazing how pressing a spray can sets off molecules designed to "capture" smelly ones, keeping them from reaching your nose. A refined little trick to improve the atmosphere, tinkering with the way our brain perceives scents.

The Hidden Crystals in Your Towel

If your towel feels like cardboard after drying, blame minerals and soap residues trapped in the fibers. When water evaporates, these residues stiffen the fabric. A rinse with warmer water or a splash of vinegar can restore softness. A small tweak to your laundry routine can return that cozy fluffiness. Who would've guessed that behind a scratchy towel lies a hidden forest of tiny crystals? Sometimes, a minor adjustment is all it takes to bring back that welcoming cotton hug.

Mold's Hidden Playground

Your bathroom can be a party zone for mold: warm, humid, and sometimes poorly ventilated. Tiny dark spots appear where air is still and dampness prevails. Opening a window, running a fan, or wiping surfaces after a shower are simple moves to crash this fungal bash. Funny how a familiar space can host a backstage drama of invisible spores eager to settle in. Prevention is the best strategy to keep the stage clean and fresh, ensuring your bathroom remains a comfortable, mold-free nook.

Colorful Toilets and Ceramic Mastery

White toilets are the standard, symbolizing simplicity and cleanliness. Yet, some people opt for bold hues. Ceramic glaze fired at high temperatures locks in pigments and creates shiny, waterproof surfaces. Choosing a different color turns your bathroom into a small design arena. A blue or red toilet might change the mood, proving that even the most mundane object can become an expressive element. It's not just taste—it's acknowledging that everyday items can be artistic statements reflecting who we are.

The Magic of Touchless Faucets

Sensor faucets feel like a futuristic touch, but they bring practical rewards: no need to touch handles, fewer germs spread around, and less wasted water. Move your hands close, water flows; pull them away, it stops. Simple, hygienic, efficient. Once you try it, going back seems odd. What looks like a small convenience actually involves sensor technology and user-friendly design. Even the simplest chore—washing hands—can turn into a tiny tech experience that's both satisfying and sensible.

Behind the Scenes of a Smart Flush

Inside the toilet's cistern, floats and valves do a silent job. Some models have dual-flush buttons: a gentle flush for small jobs, a stronger one for bigger tasks, saving water each time. It's a neat example of engineering applied to something you do daily without a second thought. Think of it as having a water wizard hidden in the wall, dispensing just what's needed. It's a subtle reminder that even the most routine gestures can be polished by smart solutions.

Nature's Anti-Skid Trick

After a long, hot bath, your fingertips shrivel like raisins. This isn't just waterlogged skin—it's thought to be an evolutionary advantage for gripping slippery objects. Nature's own anti-skid system, perhaps inherited from ancestors who foraged in damp environments. Who knew your body had such clever functions tucked away, showing up only under certain conditions? It's fascinating that something as minor as wrinkled fingertips can tell a story of adaptation and survival from ancient times.

The Secret Grip of Anti-Slip Slippers

Anti-slip slippers aren't just random rubber. Their soles have grooves and patterns designed to increase friction on smooth, wet floors. The concept is simple: more contact area, less risk of slipping. It's so intuitive you hardly notice, yet it's thanks to these small details that you can move confidently on a damp surface. Even bathroom footwear quietly incorporates physics, making sure you stay upright and secure during your morning routine.

The Showerhead's Secret Artistry

A showerhead isn't just a piece of metal with holes. Each design aims to create distinct water patterns: a gentle rain, a focused jet, or a massaging spray. Inside, channels and nozzles are arranged to shape the flow, letting you pick a soothing cascade or a revitalizing blast. Adjusting the settings transforms your shower experience, fine-tuning it to your mood. It's another reminder that everyday objects often hide thoughtful engineering, bringing comfort to something as basic as washing.

The Hidden Shield of Your Shower Curtain

Not all shower curtains are equal. Some include antimicrobial additives or special fabrics that repel moisture, making it harder for mold to settle in. With proper ventilation and a quick wipe now and then, these curtains help keep your bathroom fresh. A small example of material science improving daily life, working behind the scenes so you don't have to wage war against tiny fungi armies. Sometimes it's about choosing a curtain that's a step ahead.

Moistened Toilet Paper

Moistened toilet paper brings a softer, fresher feel to a routine we rarely think twice about. Infused with gentle lotions, it's kinder to the skin. Certain variants are biodegradable, blending hygiene with environmental care. It's a minor luxury that transforms a mundane moment into something slightly more pleasant, proving that even the simplest necessities can evolve to meet comfort and sustainability standards. A small improvement that shows how innovation can slip into any corner of our lives.

Chapter 2:
History & Curiosities from the Past

Hygiene in Ancient Egypt

If you think ancient Egyptians barely bathed, think again. Records show that wealthier Egyptians had rudimentary "bathrooms" with simple drainage systems, and some sources suggest that nobles even bathed in donkey's milk to soften their skin. Can you imagine? Certain medical papyri list a dozen recipes for fragrant cleansing ointments. They didn't have our showers, but they understood the appeal of a clean, well-groomed body in a scorching desert where every drop of water was precious. Beyond pyramids and mummies, their quest for bodily care was surprisingly refined, a subtle art of staying fresh under the relentless sun.

Absurd Victorian Inventions

In the Victorian era, new patents popped up every week, and not all were strokes of genius. Picture a hat with a tiny water tank to mist your face on hot days, or a contraption to keep your mustache dry while sipping tea. Some invented umbrella-like gadgets to shield hats from the rain, others belts with built-in massagers to slim down without moving a muscle. Most of these contraptions never took off, but they reveal a wild creativity, where enthusiasm for innovation easily outpaced common sense. A time when inventors dared to be ridiculous just to stand out.

The Bathing Rituals of Roman Emperors

Think of Roman baths as a never-ending spa party. Emperors and senators spent hours moving from hot to warm to cold rooms, discussing politics, business, and gossip. Pliny the Younger mentions baths large enough to hold hundreds of people, with pools of scented water and expert masseurs. Sometimes banquets took place poolside, with laughter and wine flowing among the steam. This wasn't just a place to get clean—it was a social hub where deals were struck and friendships forged. Hard to imagine a more luxurious setting for relaxation and networking in the ancient world.

Writing Tools Lost Over Time

Before ballpoint pens or keyboards, writing involved all sorts of unusual tools. Mesopotamian scribes pressed reed styluses into clay tablets; in Asia, brushes on bamboo strips recorded poems and decrees. Wax tablets could be erased and reused by warming them, and medieval monks sharpened goose quills with painstaking care. Each device was a mini technological triumph of its era, turning fragile materials into carriers of knowledge. It took steady hands, patience, and a little resourcefulness. Every mark on those ancient surfaces meant bridging distances and generations through simple yet ingenious writing methods.

Tales of Spies and Invisible Inks

Imagine the King of France sending secret love messages to his mistress written in lemon juice, invisible until heated by a candle flame. Venetian diplomats in the 16th century tested milk solutions or vinegar-based mixes that revealed hidden text only with special reagents. During the Cold War, advanced invisible inks required rare chemicals to emerge. It was a risky game: if the enemy discovered your trick, you had to invent a new one. A blend of science and cunning, these invisible letters turned politics into a tale of ghosts appearing under the right conditions, a spy's whisper hidden in plain sight.

Vanished Calendars and Quirky Timekeeping

Before the Gregorian calendar reigned supreme, countless cultures had their own ways of counting days. Some added extra months to realign with the seasons, others tracked time by specific star alignments or sacred cycles. Imagine starting the new year when a particular bird migrated or a certain plant blossomed. Many of these calendars are forgotten now, but they remind us that timekeeping was once deeply tied to the environment. A poetic and practical approach, where the world itself served as a clock, telling people when to sow, celebrate, or rest, guided by nature's own rhythm.

When Barbers Were Surgeons

In the Middle Ages, one fellow in a stained apron might trim your beard, pull your teeth, and lance a boil. These "barber-surgeons" performed bloodletting to "balance humors," handled tooth extractions with crude pliers, and did minor surgeries with scissors and razors. Some fairs featured public demonstrations—bloody and not exactly pleasant, but accepted back then. The barber's red-and-white pole recalls those bloodstained bandages twirling in the breeze. It's a glimpse of a time when basic medical know-how and manual skills merged in one person, in a mix that today seems both remarkable and unsettling.

Medieval Maps with Imaginary Sea Monsters

Medieval maps were often more like illustrated storybooks than accurate navigation tools. Without proper exploration data, cartographers filled unknown areas with mythical creatures: mermaids, gigantic serpents, and beasts that could swallow entire ships. These monsters weren't mere doodles; they symbolized the fear and mystery of uncharted waters. "Here be dragons" warned sailors of terrifying unknowns. Today, those fantastical maps show how human imagination tried to make sense of what lay beyond the horizon, blending wonder, anxiety, and creativity.

Hidden Sanctuaries Beneath Ancient Pyramids

In recent years, technologies like muon tomography have hinted at unseen cavities in Egyptian pyramids, fueling the idea that secret chambers might still lie undiscovered. Some legends speak of rooms filled with scrolls or untouched sarcophagi. No concrete treasure has surfaced yet, but the notion keeps archaeologists excited. A pyramid isn't just stone blocks—it might hide passageways, corridors, and, who knows, a secret that could rewrite our history. Every anomaly detected sparks hopes and dreams of revelations waiting in the darkness beneath the ancient limestone.

Oral Hygiene in the Time of Pharaohs

Ancient Egyptians cared about their teeth. Medical papyri mention abrasive pastes made from ashes, salt, or resin, plus aromatic herbs to freshen breath. Their tools? Fibrous twigs chewed at one end, turning into a kind of natural brush. Some skeletons show wear on teeth due to these gritty mixtures. There were no fluoride toothpastes or ergonomic brushes, but the idea of a neat smile and a bearable breath was already on their minds. It's amusing to imagine aristocrats of the Nile proudly showing off cleaner teeth thanks to these rudimentary methods.

Banknotes, Shells, and Rock Salt

Before paper money and minted coins, societies traded with whatever they deemed precious: rare shells, carved stones, strings of beads. On certain Pacific islands, enormous stone disks served as currency—the bigger the rock, the greater its value, even if it never moved an inch. In Africa, salt blocks were so prized they inspired the word "salary." These odd currencies show that value was once a social agreement tied to rarity and utility, not just printed numbers. A window onto how humans assigned worth to objects, long before modern economies took shape.

The Water Clock

Before pendulums and quartz watches, there were clepsydras—water clocks measuring minutes and hours by a steady drip of water from one container to another. Some were elegantly adorned; others were quite precise for their era, controlling shifts in assemblies or rituals.

In some eastern courts, water clocks got so sophisticated they included mechanical figures moving at set intervals. Imagine a world without ticking hands, where time flowed silently. Each drop represented a moment gone forever, making the passage of time feel gentle, organic, and poetic.

The Mystery of Undeciphered Manuscripts

The Voynich manuscript is the most famous, but not the only unreadable text baffling experts. Some ancient religious scripts on palm leaves or coded alchemical records remain stubbornly incomprehensible. Researchers debate whether they're elaborate hoaxes, encoded wisdom, or forgotten languages. Their charm lies in this uncertainty: are they treasures of lost knowledge or pure fantasy? Until someone finds a key, they stand as whispers from the past that refuse to reveal themselves, reminding us that not everything in history can be neatly understood.

Secret Festivities in Forgotten Courts

In certain medieval and Renaissance courts, secret feasts took place behind closed doors. Imagine banquets where guests had to solve riddles to earn dessert, or servants dressed as mythical beings delivering exotic dishes. Some texts hint at "silent suppers" where communication was only through gestures, adding a layer of intrigue. These private celebrations don't appear in your standard history books but survive in diaries and marginal notes. They paint a vivid picture of elites who indulged in culinary theater, weaving pleasure and enigma into their power plays.

The First Modern Toilet in History

In 1596, Sir John Harington designed a flushing device for Queen Elizabeth I—an early prototype of our modern toilet. It didn't catch on immediately, but it paved the way for improvements in plumbing and sanitation. Centuries later, with proper sewer systems, the toilet became a universal comfort. Who would've guessed that a single odd contraption, initially mocked, would lead to a convenience we now take utterly for granted? A forward-looking idea that slowly transformed daily life, making hygiene easier and more dignified for billions of people.

Strange Duels and Improbable Weapons

Forget elegant swordfights. There are reports—some legendary, some half-true—of 18th-century duels fought with slings or even staged in hot-air balloons. In France, one anecdote tells of a duel settled by tossing ceramic marbles with spoons! Sometimes the combatants invented absurd rules, like fighting only while lying down or attacking blindfolded. These episodes show how pride and honor led to bizarre showdowns, more circus act than deadly combat. It's both amusing and baffling that humans once solved disputes by creating their own rules of absurd engagement.

Foods Reserved for Kings

In the Middle Ages, spices like pepper or cinnamon cost more than gold, arriving from distant lands full of peril. Chocolate, introduced from the Americas, was initially sipped by Aztec rulers before becoming a European obsession. Sugar was so rare it separated the wealthy from the poor. Royal feasts displayed peacocks served in their own plumage or impossibly intricate desserts. Each dish was a statement of power: "I can afford what you can't even imagine." Today we buy these ingredients easily, forgetting that once they were the gastronomic equivalent of a crown and scepter.

The Origin of Surnames and Vanished Professions

Many Italian surnames come from ancient trades: "Ferrari" from blacksmithing, "Fabbri" from working iron, "Marinari" from seafaring. As these jobs faded, the names remained. Each surname is a tiny museum piece, a whisper of a world where a family's identity tied directly to its work. Saying your name can be like opening an old ledger: somewhere, an ancestor forged metal, baked bread, or carried water. These silent echoes remind us that language and lineage carry fragments of lost economies and crafts.

Love Letters on Tree Leaves

In some Asian cultures, messages were once inscribed on bamboo strips or palm leaves. Imagine lovers carving declarations into a leaf that would fade with the changing seasons. No digital backups, no permanent ink—just delicate words exposed to sun and rain. There's a fragile romance in that impermanence, a confession that lives briefly before nature wipes it away. At a time when we store everything endlessly, thinking of a love letter destined to vanish feels like poetry, a gentle nod to the fleeting nature of human emotion.

Exotic and Incomprehensible Funeral Ceremonies

In parts of the Pacific, some communities placed the deceased on high towers for vultures to feed upon, returning the body to nature. In Indonesia, the Toraja periodically open their ancestors' graves, clean and redress their remains, celebrating with them as if still alive. Such rituals may seem bizarre or unsettling to us, but they reflect these peoples' beliefs and love for the departed. They challenge our standard notions of mourning and show that human attitudes toward death are as varied and creative as life itself—a reminder that what seems strange to one culture can be deeply meaningful to another.

Chapter 3:
Languages, Words & Communication

Untranslatable Words from Every Continent

Ever wonder why some languages have words so unique that it takes an entire sentence in another language to explain them? In Japanese, "Komorebi" describes sunlight filtering through leaves. In Tagalog, "Kilig" captures that thrilling tingle of new love. A linguistic study counted hundreds of such untranslatable gems scattered around the globe, tiny cultural treasures packed into a single term. Danish has "Hygge," that cozy, intimate atmosphere, while Spanish "Duende" refers to intense artistic inspiration. Each untranslatable word is a secret code, a private key to how a culture feels and thinks. Think of them as rare linguistic spices adding flavors no other language can replicate.

Proverbs with Ridiculous Origins

Some everyday sayings have origins so strange they'd make you laugh out loud. The English phrase "It's raining cats and dogs" might come from old stories of animals on rooftops washed down by violent rainstorms. A Japanese proverb hints that wisdom springs from "the touch of an empty gourd," supposedly coined by a farmer after a bizarre misinterpretation centuries ago. Researchers have cataloged over 10,000 proverbs with roots so odd they sound made up by a drunk storyteller on New Year's Eve. Each saying is a linguistic souvenir linking distant worlds, a sonic puzzle made of ancient errors, superstitions, and quirky tales.

Lost Punctuation Marks

Imagine showing sarcasm with a dedicated punctuation mark, or blending a question and exclamation point into one symbol. In the past, people tried: the "interrobang" (‽) combined excitement and inquiry, but never caught on. Some languages toyed with marks for irony or rhetorical pauses. In the 18th century, a French typographer proposed a "point d'ironie," but it never gained traction. A Cambridge study found marginal notes in old manuscripts featuring strange marks—maybe unadopted prototypes. These phantom punctuations are like linguistic comets that streaked by without leaving a trail, reminding us how our writing system could've evolved into something more playful.

Alphabets Vanished Over the Centuries

Did you know entire alphabets remain unread by anyone alive today? Linear A of the Minoans still defies linguists and computers. In parts of Asia, inscriptions exist in scripts never seen elsewhere. One 2019 study estimated over 200 writing systems have vanished. If tomorrow someone cracked one of these codes, we might uncover ancient laws, lost recipes, or epic poems unread for millennia. Each unknown alphabet is like a locked treasure chest at the bottom of the ocean: we know it's there, but we can't open it. Decoding just one could rewrite whole chapters of human history.

Worlds Forged by Words

Esperanto, created in 1887, aimed to unite humanity with a neutral, easy language. Today, about two million people use it, some even writing novels in it. Klingon, invented for Star Trek, includes technical terms suited to interstellar warriors. Experts say dozens of new constructed languages are born each year as a hobby for enthusiasts. Each one is a linguistic playground, testing the boundaries of human communication. Imagine chatting in a language you invented yourself, known only to a handful of people worldwide. That's like playing linguistic gods, shaping entire worlds with fresh words and rules.

Medieval Ciphers and Secret Messages

In the Middle Ages, royal messengers carried letters that looked harmless but concealed text in invisible ink, revealed only by special reagents or heat. A 15th-century chronicle mentions a code so complex that a cryptographer took three months to solve it, earning a hefty reward in silver coins. Some codes used star charts or musical notes to mask political deals or escape plans. Cracking them meant changing a kingdom's fate. It was a silent contest of wits, where a missing vowel could rewrite history. Today, these encrypted pages feel like dusty detective stories waiting for a final solution.

The Funny Origin of Some Place Names

Certain towns have such bizarre names that tourists travel miles just to snap a photo of the sign. "Truth or Consequences" in the U.S. owes its name to a radio quiz show. In Europe, one village's name translates to "Onion Marsh Hill," supposedly coined after a medieval accident with a cart of rotten vegetables. In Australia, a surveyor's drunken mistake led to a town's nonsensical name. Each place name is a clue— a giggle in geographic form—reminding us that behind the map's labels lurk tales stranger than a comedy script.

Alphabetic Acrobatics

"The quick brown fox jumps over the lazy dog" is the famous English pangram using every letter of the alphabet. Pangrams are like linguistic acrobatics, beloved by typographers and language nerds. Some enthusiasts spend hours creating the shortest, most meaningful pangrams possible. It's a puzzle where each letter must appear at least once. Think of pangrams as alphabetic challenges, playful micro-labs that reveal hidden potentials in our everyday letters. A nerdy hobby, perhaps, but proof that even the simplest building blocks of language can be turned into sparkling verbal fireworks.

Dying Dialects Every Two Weeks

Every two weeks, a language disappears, taking with it a universe of stories, myths, and unique terms. Experts predict that by 2100, half of the 7,000 languages spoken today may vanish. With them, we lose untranslatable concepts and ways of structuring thought. It's like watching a silent library burn down, erasing priceless linguistic artworks forever. Linguists race against time to record at least some traces—audio, video, transcripts—before the last speaker is gone. Each lost dialect shrinks humanity's cultural DNA, making our global tapestry a bit thinner and paler.

Borrowed Words from Other Languages

Our languages are buffets of borrowed terms: "sushi," "taco," "computer," "barbecue." Studies show that in English, over 40% of the vocabulary has foreign origins. Italian, English, Spanish, French—they all swap words like collectors trading rare stamps. Each borrowed word is a cultural handshake, a living memory of trade routes, conquests, movies, music, or culinary encounters. It's a worldwide marketplace of sounds, flavors, and ideas, making our dictionaries richer and more vibrant.

The Secret Language of Market Vendors

In some Middle Eastern or Latin American bazaars, vendors whisper coded words to colleagues, passing secret info invisible to customers. A phrase about "three eggplants for Uncle Cat" might mean "Watch out, that buyer haggles a lot." A quick whistle pattern signals a wealthy client approaching. These hidden tongues vanish when the market closes, like fireworks at dawn. They're oral treasures, tiny linguistic galaxies lit up for a few hours, then gone without a trace. A fascinating reminder that human ingenuity bends words to its needs, even in everyday trade.

When Sound Changes Meaning

In Chinese, "ma" can mean "mother," "horse," "insult," or "hemp," depending on the tone. It's like having a verbal piano: same key, different melodies. A native speaker instantly senses the shift; a foreigner might struggle for years. Tones turn speech into a music score where pitch and inflection change the story. This acoustic artistry proves languages aren't just logical tools—they're intricate instruments, blending music and meaning in a single breath.

Whistled Languages and Remote Tribes

On the hills of La Gomera in the Canary Islands, people "speak" by whistling. It's a code that carries messages over valleys and forests. Anthropologists measured how these whistled words travel across kilometers, allowing farmers to "talk" to each other without moving. It's not just an oddity—other regions in Turkey or Mexico have similar systems. Imagine ordering dinner or warning a neighbor from afar with simple whistles. It's a reminder that human communication can exploit every resource, turning a hillside into a natural telephone line.

The Global Journey of "Ciao"

"Ciao" started in Venetian as "s-ciào," literally "I am your servant," a sign of deep respect. Over time, it morphed into a friendly, casual greeting used worldwide. Some cultures embraced it as is, adding a hint of Italian flair. This metamorphosis is like a time-traveling word: from humble submission in old Venice to a cheerful "Hi!" in cafés from New York to Rio. A single salutation that crossed oceans and centuries, shedding old meanings and adopting new faces, proving that even a common greeting can carry hidden stories.

Hand Gestures with Different Meanings Everywhere

A thumbs-up is "OK" in many places but can be an insult elsewhere. The "come here" gesture might be sweet in one country and rude in another. An anthropologist counted over 200 easily misunderstood gestures worldwide. It's astonishing that a simple movement of the hand can shift your fate in a foreign land. We imagine gestures as universal signs, but there's no global body language dictionary. Each gesture speaks its own dialect of the human body's silent conversation.

The Longest Word in a Dictionary

Some words are so long they resemble alphabetic monsters. English boasts "pneumonoultramicroscopicsilicovolcanoconiosis," a lung disease linked to inhaling fine dust. These super-long terms are often created just to impress or amuse, linguistic oddities that break records rather than serve daily needs. No one uses them in a normal chat, but their mere existence makes us grin and marvel at how far we can stretch language. Like verbal skyscrapers, they're here to show off what letters can do when piled sky-high.

Mysterious Signs and Symbols Carved in Stone

Scattered across remote cliffs and rock faces are petroglyphs—human figures, geometric patterns, and what might be star maps. Some researchers think they were calendars or spiritual codes. In one case, a modern scholar spent years trying to link certain carvings to constellations unknown to us. Without a guide, these images remain ancient riddles carved in stone. It's like finding prehistoric text messages left for future readers who never arrived. A puzzle frozen in time, waiting for a key that might never come.

Military Codes That Remain Unbroken

In wartime, armies devised ciphers so intricate they still resist modern decryption. Myths circulate about a code locked away in secret archives, possibly holding audacious war plans that never materialized. Some historians suspect it outlines strategies so daring they'd read like science fiction. The fact that no one today can crack it only heightens the allure. It's a mental treasure chest hiding in plain sight, proof that human cunning sometimes outsmarts even our cutting-edge computers.

The Language of Flowers: Silent Messages in Blooms

In 19th-century Europe, a bouquet could deliver insults or confessions. Jasmine for sweetness, chrysanthemums signaling sorrow, or roses mixed with scarlet tulips to scream passion. Without uttering a word, a person could apologize, flirt, or challenge a rival. It was a floral telegram of feelings, each petal a syllable of a scented language. Imagine receiving a bunch of violets and understanding instantly that someone whispers kindness or regret through colors and shapes. A secret dialogue blooming softly on a windowsill.

Onomatopoeia Changing Across Cultures

In Italy, a rooster goes "chicchirichì," in Germany "kikeriki," in Korea "ko-ko-dae." Not even animal sounds are universal. A researcher recorded over 300 global variations of a dog's bark! This proves that not even the simplest noises are heard identically. Each language "draws" the world's soundtrack with its own phonetic brushes, painting reality with personalized auditory colors. It's a playful reminder that language isn't just logical—it's emotional, subjective, and endlessly creative, turning the common sound of a bird or a storm into a chorus of cultural interpretations.

Chapter 4:
Nature, Animals & Extraordinary Plants

Animals That Glow in the Dark

Ever seen a beach at night lit by tiny blue sparks, like LEDs scattered across the waves? Some plankton glow chemically when disturbed. In the deep sea, about 70% of marine species have light-emitting organs: a Monterey Bay Aquarium Research Institute study confirmed that fish, jellies, and squid "light bulbs" use their glow to lure prey or charm mates. In 2018, biologists filmed a rare green-glowing worm in a South American forest, a natural disco under the roots. Each bioluminescent flash is secret code, turning darkness into a surprising stage of living light.

Carnivorous Plants Beyond Imagination

If you think plants are dull, consider that Kew Gardens botanists counted over 600 carnivorous species! The Nepenthes rajah in Borneo can trap small mammals in nectar-filled pitchers; Drosera filiformis snares insects with sticky tentacles like a leafy superhero. A Venus flytrap snaps on a fly in just 100 milliseconds—faster than a blink. These "insect-eating" plants flip our idea of vegetation as passive: they're cunning traps, ruthless and brilliant, turning nutrient-poor soil into a protein feast. It's a secret banquet right before our eyes, redefining what "rooted" life can do.

Insect Architects: Astonishing Nests and Hives

In the African desert, termites build mud towers over three meters tall, with natural air-conditioning systems beating some human designs. Researchers measured these mounds and found near-constant internal temperatures, day and night. Bees craft wax honeycombs of perfect hexagons—the ideal shape for storing honey and brood with minimal material. A biomimicry expert compares these insect constructions to "masterpieces of natural engineering." Think about it: tiny creatures, no degrees in architecture, often surpass our best solutions with timeless precision. They show that nature's engineers have been refining their art for millions of years.

Flowers That Smell Like Corpses

The Amorphophallus titanum, towering up to three meters, emits the stench of rotting flesh to attract carrion-loving insects. The Rafflesia arnoldii, over a meter wide, also "perfumes" the air with decay. Gardens worldwide see crowds lining up to smell the world's worst botanical odor. A University of Missouri study found these flowers produce volatile molecules mirroring corpse odors to lure unsuspecting pollinators. It's foul marketing genius: bugs think they've found a banquet, but end up ferrying pollen instead. A repulsive seduction trick that turns disgust into reproductive success.

Birds That Mimic Cellphone Ringtones

In Australia, the superb lyrebird copies car alarms, phone ringtones, even chainsaw buzz. A Queensland researcher recorded one lyrebird imitating 20 different urban sounds. It's not a joke: these birds use vocal creativity to impress females or claim territory. In Africa, the African grey parrot can mimic words from the radio. Such adaptability blurs the line between nature and culture. Your garden could become a stage where alarms, pop jingles, and beeps transform into love songs. Birds remix our noisy world into their personal soundtrack, surprising us with every note.

Fish That Walk on Land

The mudskipper crawls out of the water and "walks" on mud using its fins as tiny legs. A scientist timed its trek onshore, finding it survives hours in open air. Some African lungfish endure months buried in dried mud, breathing air until rain returns. It's like traveling back in time to when vertebrates first stepped onto land. These amphibious fish ignore boundaries between water and earth, proving evolution's infinite imagination. They bridge worlds, a "wow" moment of adaptation that shatters our idea of what fish "should" be.

Mammals That Lay Eggs

The platypus is a natural collage: duck bill, beaver tail, otter-like body, webbed feet—and it lays eggs. Males have a venomous spur, too! When shown to British scientists in 1799, they suspected a prank. Yet it's real: a mammal defying categories, blending features from birds and reptiles. Genetic analyses revealed it shares genes with multiple lineages. It's as if nature pulled random parts from a box and created a one-of-a-kind creature. A living contradiction, the platypus challenges neat labels and reminds us evolution enjoys playing wild cards.

Giant Underground Fungi

Some fungi form massive organisms sprawling across kilometers underground. Armillaria ostoyae in Oregon covers about 9 square kilometers, considered one of Earth's largest living beings. A single fungal network can live for millennia, acting like a "Wood Wide Web" linking roots of different plants. Invisible from above, this giant silent empire exchanges nutrients and information. A super-organism of resilience and patience, mocking our notions of size and lifespan. A colossal hidden kingdom beneath our feet, ancient and enduring, quietly shaping forest life over countless centuries.

Monkeys Stealing Your Sunglasses

In certain Bali temples, monkeys pilfer sunglasses, hats, and phones from tourists. A University of Lethbridge study observed that monkeys pick valuable objects first, then wait for humans to offer food in exchange. It's a clever extortion racket: the higher the item's worth, the more "ransom" they demand. Almost a black market in the treetops, forcing embarrassed tourists to bargain with crafty primates. This skill shows cognitive agility emerging unexpectedly, mixing animal cunning and human frustration into a daily comedy.

The Chameleon's Secret

Chameleons don't just shift colors to vanish into leaves; it's also a visual language to express mood, stress, dominance, or romance. A research team filmed chameleons adjusting patterns in seconds, mapping emotional states onto their skin. Some males flaunt psychedelic hues to impress females, while a frightened one darkens to repel rivals. Not mere camouflage, but a living stage of colors. A cutaneous theater revealing a complex social code, proving nature isn't mute but speaks with pigments, light, and intricate displays.

The World's Oldest Trees

A bristlecone pine in the U.S. surpasses 4,800 years: already old when pyramids rose in Egypt. A spruce in Sweden, with 9,500-year-old roots, witnessed ice ages and vanished empires. Tree rings are pages in a climatic diary: reading them is like flipping through epochs. Scientists call these ancient trees "silent witnesses," storing stories of storms and droughts. Imagine a being that outlives entire civilizations, unmovable and wise. It's a humbling "wow" that redefines our sense of time, showing that a plant can survive the grand narratives of human history.

Forests That Communicate Underground

Plants aren't isolated: mycorrhizal fungi link their roots, enabling sugar trades and chemical messages. A stressed tree can send nutrients to a nearby "offspring." Canadian researchers filmed signals passing through soil networks, like a green social network. It's a quiet cooperation, not just competition, a hidden internet of roots and fungi. Picture a woodland as a caring community, where neighbors support each other without words. This silent concert of exchanges and alliances reshapes our vision of nature as a theater of constant, mutual help.

Marine Creatures That Don't Age

The Turritopsis dohrnii jellyfish "resets" itself to a juvenile stage, potentially forever, earning the nickname "immortal jellyfish." Scientists wonder if unraveling its DNA might reveal secrets of aging. Some Arctic clams live over 500 years without obvious senescence. These beings bend or even ignore the rules of time. Hidden beneath the waves are life forms that toy with mortality. It's beyond our wildest sci-fi: creatures that mock the ticking clock, inspiring questions about life's fundamental rules.

Deserts in Bloom

The Atacama, one of Earth's driest deserts, occasionally erupts into a carnival of flowers after rare rainfalls. Seeds sleep underground for years, waking after a few drops of moisture. Within hours, a drab land transforms into a painter's palette. Photographers and botanists rush to witness this ephemeral miracle. Two weeks later, it's all gone. A seasonal rainbow, proof that life bides its time, waiting patiently to explode into color. A reminder never to underestimate even the harshest environments, where beauty lurks under the sand, ready to dazzle.

Rodents as Shiny Collectors

Some rodents hoard glossy objects like tiny jewelers. Ecologists observed mice gathering colorful seeds and iridescent shell fragments, seemingly decorative items without nutritional value. Perhaps a ploy to impress mates or mark territory. It's like discovering a mini art gallery in their burrows. This aesthetic sense in small mammals defies our assumptions. They aren't just eating and breeding machines; they're mini curators, adding unexpected flair to their homes. A hidden charm that shows nature's subtle inventiveness.

The Wolf's Howl

A wolf pack's howl isn't random noise. It coordinates hunts, reunites lost members, and sets territorial boundaries. Zoologists analyzed recordings showing a wolf can modulate its voice to sound like several wolves, bluffing rivals. Some ethologists suspect wolves recognize individual "accents" of packmates. Not just a spooky "awoo," but a sophisticated acoustic code. Knowing this, the chorus of a winter night's howl becomes a secret council meeting, an exchange of data and strategy. It's a revelation that turns a cliché of wilderness into a symphony of cunning and cooperation.

Bacteria Thriving in Volcanoes

In boiling springs and sulfuric vapors where everything else would perish, certain bacteria flourish. Biologists isolated strains enduring 120°C, feeding on metals and sulfur. Called "extremophiles," they challenge biochemical limits. Some dream of harnessing their enzymes for industry, or find clues for life on Mars. Who knew that in these hellish cauldrons lurked organisms that laugh at our comfort zone? It proves life's tenacity: even in infernos, evolution sets up camp, leaving us marveling at its fearless grit.

Butterflies Migrating with Incredible Routes

Monarch butterflies travel over 4,000 km from Canada to Mexico, crossing entire countries. They rely on ancient instincts, sun angles, and magnetic fields. Scientists fitted tiny sensors on some monarchs and discovered astonishing precision year after year. Imagine a fragile orange-and-black traveler performing an epic odyssey, a relay race of generations. Each delicate flap propels them through storms, highways, and deserts. A natural GPS no human can match. Their journey humbles us, reminding us that navigation can be coded into fragile wings, lighting a spark of wonder in our rational minds.

Pink Lakes and Rainbow Oceans

Lake Hillier in Australia shines shocking pink, thanks to special algae and bacteria. Some tropical seas glow in neon blues and greens from bioluminescent plankton. Mineral-rich ponds in other regions display surreal oranges and purples. Around the globe, researchers counted at least 50 vividly hued lakes, each with unique chemistry. It's as if nature wields a psychedelic paintbrush, defying the notion that water must be blue. Each colorful aquatic spectacle is a cosmic wink, a reminder that the palette of Earth's waters can stun us with unexpected artistry.

Dancing Bees: Choreographies of Coordinates

Bees show other foragers where to find flowers by dancing. A figure-eight waggle and the angle of the dance relative to the sun convey distance and direction. An entomologist discovered that dance duration equals meters to fly, and orientation sets the course. Without GPS, these winged farmers share detailed info through a ballet. A coded show so efficient and elegant that it redefines how we see insects. Picture a hive as a dance floor where every step is a crucial instruction. A visual opera of legs and vibrations that makes gathering nectar a communal, graceful endeavor.

Chapter 5:
Food Cooking and Curious Eating Habits

Honey That Never Dies

Not a myth: honey found in 3,000-year-old Egyptian tombs was still edible. This amber nectar, crafted by tireless bees, endures for centuries due to its low moisture and acidic pH, both unfriendly to bacteria. An archaeologist once described a jar found near a pharaoh's mummy, perfectly preserved. Lab tests show minimal alterations over decades. Picture it as a sweet time capsule crossing millennia without spoiling. A kind of immortal food that mocks the calendar and allows today's palate to taste ancient sweetness.

Fruits From a World of Wonders

If you think you know all fruits, you are underestimating nature's imagination. Durian, adored in Asia, smells like rotten onions but offers a vanilla custard flavor. Pitaya, the "dragon fruit," reveals fuchsia pulp studded with black seeds, gentle as a delicate kiwi. Baobab fruit, loaded with vitamin C, comes as a powdery pulp you mix with water for a nutrient boost in Africa. An ethnobotanist found at least 50 such exotic fruits unknown to the average market. A feast of shapes and flavors beyond the usual apple, inviting you to widen your horizons.

Fermentations That Challenge Taste and Courage

Swedish surströmming, a fermented herring with a smell so intense that some open the can underwater, leaves newcomers speechless. In Japan, natto (sticky fermented soybeans) divides diners: some cherish its protein punch, others flee its gym-sock aroma. Certain blue cheeses contain hundreds of aroma molecules, a chemical concerto that can enchant or repel. One daring food blogger tested 10 extreme fermented foods and came out fascinated. These experiences remind us that good or bad flavor is cultural. Venturing into these extremes can spark love where you least expect it.

Ancient Tea Rituals That Amaze

Before tea became a quiet afternoon drink, it served as currency, medicine, even a symbol of power. In ancient China, compressed tea "bricks" traded like fragrant gold. On the Tibetan plateau, tea is mixed with yak butter and salt, a rich soup against freezing winds. Old manuals detail ceremonies where every gesture with the cup carried spiritual meaning. A specialist counted over 200 different tea rituals in Asia. More than a simple infusion, tea was once precious coin and spiritual guide, weaving economics, philosophy, and comforting warmth into a single steaming cup.

Cacao Seeds Once Worth a Fortune

Long before chocolate bars, cacao seeds were currency among Maya and Aztecs. A Spanish chronicler noted that 100 cacao beans could buy a rabbit. Considered "food of the gods," it was consumed as a bitter, spiced drink. Today, chocolate is everywhere, but back then it was a luxury for elites and warriors. A culinary anthropologist compared cacao's value to gold at certain times. From the bitter powder of ancient empires to today's sweet delight, this evolution shows how a precious seed became universal joy.

Insects on the Table a New Culinary Frontier

Toasted grasshoppers, fried larvae, chocolate-coated ants: already 2 billion people enjoy insects as food. The UN suggests insects as a sustainable protein source. An entomological foodie tasted 50 insect species, finding flavors like nuts or shrimp. While some Westerners recoil, top chefs experiment with cricket flour in pasta or bread. European markets now sell worm snacks. Resistance is cultural, not gastronomic: one brave bite might reveal a world of tastes, a ticket to the future of nourishment.

Medieval Recipes a Bizarre Feast

In the Middle Ages, court cooks served swans re-dressed in their skins, chickens painted with saffron, entire animals stuffed into others. Rare, costly spices masked off flavors. A French 14th-century cookbook listed 200 dishes now deemed "culinary oddities." It was a show of power: whoever could afford rare spices and exotic meats flaunted wealth. Modern "archeo-chefs" tried reviving a sweet-and-salty medieval soup and found it intriguing. Back then, every meal was a performance, the table a stage of gastronomic wonders that might shock today's palates but still fascinate.

Foods That Change Flavor When Observed

A psychological test served two identical juices: one colorless, one dyed red. Most tasters found the red juice sweeter. Research shows that visual cues reshape taste perception. In one famous trial, white wine tinted red fooled even expert sommeliers. It's the mind's power: we "season" foods with our eyes first. No longer just a matter of taste buds, flavor involves the gaze. A dance of senses where color acts as a hidden ingredient, turning the plate into a canvas that deceives and delights.

Sushi a Legend Reinvented Through Time

Today's sushi is minimal and refined, but its ancestors were fish fermented in rice for months, yielding sour and pungent flavors. Over time, vinegar replaced long fermentation, bringing freshness to the fore. A food historian notes that sushi's journey from preserved fish to elegant morsel reflects centuries of adaptation. The modern nigiri, delicate and neat, would shock an ancient diner. Sushi's story proves that cuisine evolves, reinterprets itself, and serves a bite of history with every piece.

Camel Milk and Unexpected Dairy Discoveries

Not only cows: in Central Asia, camel milk rich in vitamin C fuels energy drinks against desert climates. In parts of Africa, donkey milk is filtered through plant fibers for unique cheeses. In the Himalayas, yak butter enriches salty Tibetan tea. The FAO estimates that at least 10% of global milk comes from non-bovine sources. Every community domesticates what's available, shaping flavors and nutrients. A collective manual of human ingenuity: where cows are scarce, reindeer or goats step in, feeding remote populations with resourcefulness.

Sparkling Drinks Born From Flowers

Before commercial sodas, some communities fermented elderflowers, herbs, or honey for lightly fizzy beverages. Mead, enjoyed by ancient Germanic tribes, was a "sparkling" delight of the past. Historians discovered millennia-old flower-based syrup recipes, naturally effervescent thanks to wild yeasts. Sipping these floral elixirs is like tasting a garden in a bottle. Today, craft breweries rediscover these formulas, offering subtle bubbles and ancient flavors. Each sip holds seasons and pollen, a toast to rural roots gently revived for modern palates.

Record Hot Peppers a Flame to Challenge

The Carolina Reaper exceeds 2 million Scoville units, a gauntlet for spicy daredevils. In Mexico, chili-eating contests see warriors sweating, crying, and laughing at their own bravery. Capsaicin, the irritant compound, tricks pain receptors. Compared to an average chili, these firebombs are 100 times hotter. It's a dance of agony and pleasure, a culinary rite of passage. The chili transcends seasoning, becoming a badge of honor. Who endures the burn stands tall, proving courage with a single bite.

Sacred Foods and Rituals by the Fire

Around the globe, certain dishes prepared in religious ceremonies carry transcendent meaning. In parts of the Amazon, eating together around a fire and invoking ancestors weaves present and past. In India, pouring ghee into a holy flame connects the earthly to the divine. A food anthropologist counted hundreds of rituals where meals become spiritual messages. Not just calories, but codes for the cosmos, plates that whisper to gods through grains and seeds. Culinary acts become prayers, each ingredient a syllable in a language of flame and faith.

Pasta and Pizza Myths to Debunk

No, Marco Polo didn't bring pasta from China: Italian records predate that tale. Modern pizza with tomato and mozzarella took shape in 19th-century Naples, not in ancient times. A culinary historian shows that post–World War II American soldiers in Italy helped globalize pizza. Beloved dishes we think eternal are actually recent inventions. Knowing the true origins adds flavor to every bite, stripping away clichés and revealing the real journeys of our favorite foods.

Space Cuisine Beyond Tubes and Purées

Early astronauts sucked puréed foods from tubes. Today's spacefarers enjoy freeze-dried pasta, chocolate bars, and even artisan espresso. Chefs and nutritionists design menus for zero gravity, ensuring taste and variety survive orbit. NASA studies show spicy condiments help counter reduced smell and taste in space. Each bite up there is a comfort reminder of home, a flavorful anchor in silent vacuum. Gastronomy follows humans beyond Earth, seasoning the stars with familiar warmth.

Savory Smoothies and Surprising Blends

Not all smoothies are sweet. Some nations blend tomato, garlic, and fermented fish into savory drinks. A gastro-anthropologist listed dozens of "salty shakes" in Africa and Latin America. In Mexico, a bar famous for chili-vegetable blends serves this "liquid snack" as refreshing fuel. These beverages smash taste boundaries, proving that sweetness isn't mandatory. One sip and your mind rebels, then opens to new frontiers. It's an invitation to laugh at habits, embracing strangeness as part of the culinary landscape.

Glutamate the Truth Behind the Myth

Long demonized, MSG is no more dangerous than other additives. Recent studies refute the "Chinese Restaurant Syndrome." Glutamate enhances umami, that "savory" taste identified last century. Even tomatoes have natural glutamate! Blind tests show adding MSG boosts satisfaction by about 30%. It's proof that culinary fears often stem from misinformation. Understanding the science behind this molecule dismantles biases. A relief for curious palates, ready to celebrate the fifth taste with open arms.

The Potato a History Rich in Mysteries

The potato came from South America and faced suspicion in Europe, once thought strange and poisonous. Yet it saved entire populations from famine. An economist estimated potato cultivation increased Europe's agricultural output by 25%. From initial distrust to global staple, the potato's journey shows how cross-continental encounters create culinary pillars. Every fry, every mash carries echoes of explorers, farmers, and survival stories. A humble tuber turned hero, rewriting menus worldwide.

Gelatinized Foods and Curious Past Trends

In the '50s, encapsulating foods in vibrant gelatin meant modernity. Eggs, meat, and veggies suspended in translucent blocks dazzled home cooks. A culinary archive reveals hundreds of these "jelly" recipes. Today, we find them odd, but then they symbolized innovation—a centerpiece that shone like edible sculpture. Revisiting vintage photos is like entering a gastronomic museum of strangeness.

Taste evolves: what was chic yesterday seems kitsch now, a reminder that the dining table follows fleeting fashions as readily as the runway.

Ancestral Broths With a Hint of Magic

Before modern supplements, broths of bones, algae, or roots fortified warriors and peasants. Japanese samurai sipped miso broth for courage; European shepherds boiled hearty soups against the cold. A nutritionist found these ancient broths packed with minerals, proteins, and anti-inflammatory properties. Not just comfort food, but a liquid balm handed down through generations. A spoonful revives old rituals, a warm hug from distant centuries. Even now, as we taste a simple chicken soup, we sense an echo of ancestors fighting frost and fatigue with the same steamy elixir of well-being.

Chapter 6:
Arts and Entertainment

Paintings Made With Unexpected Pigments

Some artists skip traditional paints and choose outrageous materials: coffee, wine, even blood or soil. A Brazilian painter uses cocoa powder for warm tones and a sweet fragrance. An Australian artist experimented with red wine, creating hues that evolve as the liquid ages. In 2017, a Japanese performer painted a mural with squid ink, turning the gallery into an "aquatic atelier." In France, a museum displayed works made from diamond dust, rare and radiant. These creators reinvent the palette, proving that ingenuity can color the world with the most unlikely substances.

Musical Instruments Built From Scrap

In Brazilian favelas or African townships, orchestras emerge from discarded barrels, pipes, and metal scraps. A violin from a tin can, a double bass from an empty oil drum, guitars from old electrical wires. The Recycled Orchestra of Cateura in Paraguay grew famous: young musicians turning landfill debris into melodies. They recorded albums, toured internationally. The message is clear: music knows no limits, not even poverty. Where there is no money, creativity strings together harmonies, transforming trash into hopeful symphonies and showing that art can flourish in the humblest places.

Sand Sculptures That Challenge Time

On beaches, some artists sculpt sand into fairy-tale castles or lifelike portraits. Masters of this craft might add natural resins so the creations last for weeks. In 2019, an Indian artist carved a six-meter Buddha in sand, drawing thousands of onlookers. International competitions judge anatomical precision in these sandy faces as if it were a top-tier art biennial. Yet rain or wind can erase them in a day. This is art at its most ephemeral, a dance with nature's clock, reminding us that beauty can be as fleeting as a wave on the shore.

Silent Cinema Hiding Secret Sounds Behind the Scenes

Early silent films were not truly silent: in theaters, a pianist played live, and a sound-effects person created noises with random objects. Some venues hired small orchestras. In 1920s London, a cinema featured a talented violinist and a man who clicked walnut shells to mimic footsteps. In Japanese halls, a benshi storyteller narrated plots and gave voices to characters. A researcher uncovered old musician contracts that prove these invisible sounds were crucial. Rediscovering this audio backdrop reveals another dimension of cinematic magic, where silence was actually brimming with life's whispers.

Art Installations Drifting on Icebergs

Contemporary artists sometimes place temporary sculptures on Arctic icebergs, aware that melting will soon reclaim them. A mask carved in ice sailed through Canadian fjords for days before dissolving. A Nordic collective uses drones to fix colored fabrics onto floating blocks. An ephemeral gallery, reminding us that art can appear and vanish like ice under the sun, pushing viewers to chase creations and embrace impermanence. These adventurous projects blend aesthetics and ecological messages, proving beauty can bloom even in icy realms where time and nature hold absolute power.

Modern Puppeteers Weaving Ancient Tales

Puppet theater isn't just kid's entertainment: in some Eastern cultures it recounts millennia-old myths, historical dramas, and political themes. Indonesian wayang kulit silhouettes cast shadows on a white screen, bringing heroes and demons to life. In Tuscany, a master puppeteer adapts local legends with hand-carved puppets. Festivals celebrate international marionette artistry, merging old epics and new stories. These wooden and fabric performers prove that art speaks through invisible hands, connecting past and present, and turning a simple stage into a bridge between eras, languages, and memories.

Photography Without a Camera

Some artists create images without lenses. They place objects on photosensitive paper and expose it to light, producing a photogram. This early 19th-century technique yields dreamy silhouettes and abstract contrasts. Avant-garde artists in the 20th century experimented with lace, leaves, even newspaper cutouts. Today, a few photographers revisit the photogram as pure expression, no digital gimmicks. One critic calls them "light imprints," where a simple flower pressed onto paper becomes poetic geometry. This lens-free approach reminds us that image-making can flow from elemental encounters of light and substance.

Hidden Theaters in Unimaginable Places

Theater performances sprout in abandoned factories, old mines, defunct buses, or underpasses. Bold troupes turn improbable spaces into stages. An Italian company once staged Hamlet in a shopping mall parking lot, surprising unsuspecting shoppers. A French group performs monologues on a boat in a canal, while the audience watches from shore. These shows transform ordinary corners into extraordinary scenes, blurring the line between daily life and drama. One urban art expert says these events awaken imagination, forcing us to see the city anew, where every corner might cradle a story waiting to unfold.

Murals That Come Alive With Optical Illusions

Murals are no longer just paint on a wall: some artists create 3D effects and perspective tricks that look like portals to other worlds. In Brazil, a painter transformed steps into a convincing waterfall if viewed from the right angle. In Paris, interactive graffiti change appearance with daylight, using natural shadows to reveal hidden subjects. Street art becomes a conversation with space, involving the viewer in a visual riddle. These works show how art can turn a blank façade into a stage for illusions, opening imaginary windows onto the possible.

Bizarre Comics From Distant Cultures

Not only Japanese manga or American comics exist—unusual graphic narratives thrive in unexpected places. In parts of Africa, cartoonists depict mythical creatures unknown elsewhere; in Peru, they revive pre-Columbian legends. An Indian "comic architect" experiments with unconventional speech bubbles and panel layouts, breaking Western traditions. These authors blend art, oral history, and local influences, shaping unknown graphic worlds. Browsing such a volume lets us discover far-off identities through drawings and text. Each new comic proves that image-based storytelling can be reborn endlessly, different and surprising every time.

Performances Where the Audience Becomes the Star

Why remain a seated spectator? Some immersive shows make viewers participants. Interactive installations, "walking theater" in the streets, or house-based narratives where guests decide the plot's outcome. In one London show, the audience receives clues and objects, building the story together with the cast. A New York director asked spectators to dance with the actors, erasing the performer-viewer gap. Art becomes a shared experience, where everyone helps shape an unrepeatable moment. The stage expands beyond the set, transforming us all into co-authors of a living performance.

Artists Who Paint Using Unusual Body Parts

Artists without arms paint with their feet or mouth, proving talent can conquer physical limits. One in Asia creates huge canvases with only his feet, producing precise, harmonious strokes. An international association of artists without hands sells their works in renowned museums. This isn't pity; it's a celebration of ingenuity. The entire body becomes a brush, defying stereotypes about who "can" create art. Each painting is a lesson in willpower. Their exhibitions move and inspire, showing that passion for art breaks every barrier.

The Oldest Graffiti Made by Humankind

Prehistoric cave art, scratched into stone millennia ago, can be seen as ancestral graffiti. Simplified animals, human figures, and abstract symbols formed messages before writing existed. A paleoanthropologist discovered 70,000-year-old paintings in South Africa: maybe hunt scenes, maybe sacred signs. Like today's urban murals, they were free expressions, beyond galleries or rules, testifying the timeless human need to depict thoughts and feelings. A silent dialogue between distant epochs, where rock walls become the first pages of an endless tale.

Rare Vinyl Records and Extreme Collectors

Some collectors spend thousands of dollars for a rare vinyl record pressed in just a few copies. A 1959 jazz LP sold at auction for mind-blowing sums. They travel the globe hunting a single track recorded half a century ago. Think of them as sound explorers, eager to grasp a musical fragment of history. For them, vinyl is more than just sound; it's a relic, a precious artifact. The music becomes tangible heritage, each record a piece of cultural DNA spun on a turntable, unlocking memories and distant echoes.

Films Shot Within a Single Room

Bold directors have filmed entire movies confined to one space—a living room, a cellar. Without shifting scenery, the story relies on dialogue, expressions, and subtle details. A famous filmmaker said the constraint sparks creativity: no grand landscapes, no effects, just tension in minimal form. The audience focuses on glances, whispers, lighting shifts. Without spectacular backdrops, each gesture gains importance. These minimalist sets turn films into exercises in pure narrative tension, proving that a four-walled stage can hold a universe of emotions.

Marionettes Dancing on Water

In Vietnam, a centuries-old tradition stages puppet shows on ponds and lakes. Painted figures—dragons, fish, farmers—move across watery stages, controlled by puppeteers wading waist-deep, hidden behind screens. Accompanied by local instruments, these watery ballets were once rural entertainment, now popular attractions. Maneuvering strings and rods under the surface demands skill, making each movement fluid and enchanting. A cultural historian calls it "amphibious opera," blending tradition, music, and clever engineering. Audiences see a symphony of reflections and ripples, an aquatic dream world come to life.

Endless Concerts That Break Records

Some musical performances last days, weeks, even years. A German church organ plays a John Cage composition designed to stretch 639 years. Elsewhere, bands attempt 24-hour marathons for charity. Experimental festivals propose infinite sessions, where music flows like a sonic river. Spectators come and go, witnessing a living sound installation. These extremes challenge the idea that music must be brief. Instead, they open a timeless dimension, where sound becomes a landscape and the listener a wanderer in a never-ending melody.

Poems Written Backward to Puzzle the Mind

Some poets craft verses legible only in a mirror or reversed text, forcing readers to decode a riddle. A French poet once sent a "mirror poem" manuscript to a publisher, earning confusion and rejection. But it's not a prank: flipping words forces the reader into creative effort. It's like a literary puzzle that expands the page's boundaries. Those who decode it discover fresh meaning and perspectives. Such works prove that literature can play with form, not just content, and spark intellectual gymnastics for those willing to read in reverse.

Theatrical Costumes Stitched From Recycled Materials

In an age of sustainability, visionary costume designers use recycled plastic, cardboard, and old sheets. An opera in London dressed its cast in bottle-cap hats and newspaper skirts. This approach turns waste into sartorial masterpieces, merging aesthetics and ethics. The stage becomes a green showcase, teaching reuse and reinvention. When applause erupts, it's not just for actors but for creativity giving new life to scraps—an eco-lesson sewn into every garment.

Unusual Museums Devoted to the Strangest Things

There are museums for almost everything: human hair, molds, safety pins, even electric chairs. An Icelandic curator manages a museum of animal marine penises; in Japan, another displays stones resembling human faces. These absurd collections spring from eccentric passions, cataloging the unimaginable. Visiting them is entering the mind of a wildly inventive collector, witnessing the endless potential of human taste. Who would think to preserve such oddities? A trip to these places brings amused disbelief, proving that collecting can turn the bizarre into a cultural treasure trove.

Chapter 7:
Sports Games and Astonishing Records

A Mad Chase After a Rolling Cheese

On a steep English hillside, each year a wheel of Gloucester cheese is sent racing downward, with a pack of daredevils hurtling behind it, tumbling head over heels. Some roll for dozens of meters without stopping, others wear motorcycle helmets as if this were a daredevil descent. A journalist once recorded thirty falls in a single race. The winner's prize is the cheese itself, but the real reward is the instant local fame. Its origins may date back to the 18th century, proving that humans will do anything to stand out, even defying gravity and common sense, and leaving onlookers laughing in disbelief.

Soccer on Ice and the Art of Elegant Falling

Imagine a soccer match played on a frozen lake, where even star players slip around like penguins. A study on Scandinavian "ice soccer cups" noted that players keep the ball under control for mere seconds before it skids away unpredictably. Goals arise from lucky bounces rather than tactical brilliance, and the crowd laughs as skilled athletes become clumsy acrobats. Think of it as a clownish ballet on ice that topples the usual seriousness of soccer. It reminds us that sport can recover its playful spirit, making luck, not strategy, the true star of the field.

Marathons in Costume a Parade of Smiling Runners

Picture a marathon where thousands run not for speed but for fun, dressed as superheroes, giant bananas, or cartoon characters. A survey at a Spanish race found over 50% joined for the party atmosphere. Some participants break into dances mid-course, others snap selfies with competitors. One runner finished 42 kilometers dressed as an inflatable dinosaur in just over five hours. This phenomenon shatters competitive seriousness, showing how freeing the event from time pressures can turn a grueling run into a traveling carnival of laughter and color.

Underwater Chess Strategies in Apnea

In some pools, players compete in underwater chess. They wear masks and snorkels, holding their breath while moving pieces fixed on a weighted board. Each turn is a feat of calm and oxygen control. A German tournament once recorded a 15-minute match with players emerging only briefly for air. It's a surreal inversion of logic: the mind must strategize while lungs strain. The chessboard becomes a silent stage beneath the surface, blending tactics with physiology, and astonishing anyone who witnesses this aquatic duel of wits.

Hula Hoop Marathons and the Triumph of Perseverance

The hula hoop, a simple child's toy, can become an epic test of endurance. An American spinner kept it rotating over 70 hours straight, surpassing physical fatigue and boredom. The Guinness records confirm human resilience can bloom from a plastic ring. Sports psychologists note that the hypnotic repetition induces a meditative mental state, while the amazed crowd counts minutes, then hours. It leaves us stunned: if we can turn a playful hoop into a marathon challenge, then nothing is too trivial to become extraordinary.

Cars and a Ball the Absurd Motorized Match

In certain tournaments, instead of players, cars take the field to push a giant ball, a wild hybrid of bumper cars and soccer. Control dissolves into chaos: cars collide, the ball bounces unpredictably, fans roar with laughter. An event in the US drew huge crowds, proof that the line between sport and spectacle is fluid. It's less about winning than delivering a mechanical circus of noise and collisions. A sign that when skill isn't enough, we entertain with horsepower, making the audience marvel at our inventive madness.

Candy Cane Fencing a Sweet Duel

At some holiday festivals, mock tournaments replace swords with giant candy canes. Fighters end up with sticky hands and sugar-coated laughter rather than bruises. A Canadian organizer reported increasing attendance every year as families join in. It's a return to childhood games, now turned into playful "competitions." The audience claps, reminded that the boundary between sport and joke can vanish at any moment. All it takes is a colorful candy cane to conjure a new reason to smile.

Tree Climbing the Evolution of a Childhood Game

There are actual championships for climbing trees, where athletes race up trunks and leap between branches like nimble squirrels. An Australian event saw a competitor reach 20 meters high in mere seconds, scored by official judges. It's a return to nature's original playground, with bark instead of rock. Some environmentalists hope it raises awareness about forests. Who would have guessed that scaling a tree, once a child's pastime, could become a recognized discipline, a tribute to our bond with the woods?

Pillow Fights for World Records Softest Showdown Ever

Hundreds gather wielding pillows, thrashing at each other to break the world record for the largest pillow fight. Feathers swirl, laughter erupts, and no one gets hurt. A North American festival counted over 5,000 participants in a single event, turning a simple bedroom game into a media spectacle. No points, no strategy, just a gentle storm of cushions. It proves that even the simplest pastime can gain legendary status, filling a city square with fluffy chaos and collective giggles.

Global Treasure Hunts and International Quests

Not just backyard scavenger hunts: some are organized worldwide, with cryptic clues hidden across countries. In a 2019 contest, fifty teams from around the globe followed riddles leading them to obscure monuments. It's an adventure blending mystery and competition, a kind of collective Indiana Jones in a hyperconnected era. Beyond the prize, the true reward is discovering unknown places, collaborating with strangers, and feeling the thrill of global exploration. It's as if the planet becomes a giant puzzle, each clue unveiling surprise and awe.

Sports Born From Everyday Breaks and Imagination

Bossaball fuses volleyball, soccer, and trampolines; bubble football puts players in inflatable spheres. Many odd sports start as jokes among friends, invented during a coffee break. An "alternative sports" survey found that a good share of new disciplines emerge from boredom or a spark of creativity. A ball, a weird rule, and a playful mind are enough. This shows human ingenuity is boundless: everything can turn into a sport if we dare to smile and compete. A reminder that the office or the beach can birth tomorrow's bizarre champions.

Racing the Frozen Frontier

Some run marathons at -20°C, cross icy deserts, or dive into polar waters. The Antarctic Ice Marathon attracts participants from 20 nations. A sports physician observed their physiology: racing hearts, reduced oxygen intake, yet immense euphoria. Defeating extreme cold becomes a psychological medal. An astonishing spectacle, where athletes laugh in winter's face, turning harsh climates into opponents to be conquered. It's a testament to human tenacity, wrestling warmth from a hostile environment and leaving us amazed.

Sack Races Upgraded to Top-Level Competition

The old sack race from picnics can become an official tournament. Skilled competitors practice techniques to hop stable and fast, shaving off precious milliseconds. A record reports a runner covering 100 meters in under 20 seconds inside a sack. Proof that even the simplest activity can gain complexity if we add a competitive edge. The sack, symbol of childlike simplicity, becomes a tool for elite performance, making us grin at the idea that anywhere determination thrives, a sport can be born.

Bicycle on a Tightrope Nerves of Steel in Midair

Some daredevils pedal across a high wire stretched above the ground, merging circus bravery and cycling precision. A French event saw a biker cross 30 meters of cable at dizzying height, no safety net below. Spectators held their breath, aware one slip means disaster. Balancing is absolute, fear tangible. This athletic poetry of equilibrium leaves us stunned. If the human mind can guide a bicycle along a thread of steel, what else is possible? A question that sends shivers down our spine.

Cellphone Tossing Liberation Through a Throw

Tired of old phones? Some competitions have people hurling outdated cellphones as far as they can. A Finnish record surpasses 100 meters. It's not anger, but humorous freedom from outdated tech. A leisure time psychologist notes it can reduce stress. Absurd yet cathartic, turning a common gadget into a harmless projectile, a witty rejection of modern excess. Laughing at our devices by throwing them away—who would have thought?

Typing Wizards a Tribute to Speed and Precision

Before computers, typists competed to see who typed fastest on mechanical keyboards, hitting over 120 words per minute without error. It was a mechanical symphony, a forerunner of today's speed-typing challenges. The clang of keys and lightning fingers elevated office tasks to a spectacular feat of skill. This proves humans have always sought ways to surpass limits, even in what seems mundane. The tapping of letters becomes a record-breaking anthem.

Living Chess Pieces and Theatrical Showdowns

In certain squares, people dressed as chess pieces stand on a giant board. The knight is an actor who prances, the rook a towering figure, the queen a regal dame in elaborate robes. Every move is a choreographed step, every capture a tiny drama. An event in Marostica, Italy, draws thousands of tourists to watch strategy become a living play. Chess's cold logic marries colorful spectacle, leaving everyone marveling at this fusion of intellect and artistic flair.

Running Backward the World in Reverse

Some events make athletes run entire races backward. A German competitor completed a half marathon at a remarkable pace facing the wrong way. This flips our understanding of movement: muscles and senses adapt to a world turned around. The crowd laughs but also admires the skill. A visual perception researcher says running backward trains the brain to interpret reversed landscapes. A crazy idea that proves the human spirit loves overturning norms and unveiling fresh possibilities.

Beds on Wheels Racing Through Town

In a few towns, teams push wheeled beds through streets and alleys at high speed, wearing pajamas and losing pillows along the way. A festival reported huge turnouts, turning furniture into racing machines. The goal isn't just victory, but creating a folkloric show that draws tourists. Who would guess a bed, symbol of rest, could become a racing chariot? It shows that human creativity can transform domestic objects into a carnival of speed and laughter.

Dancing on Cooled Lava Testing the Extreme

Some athletes snowboard on lava slopes, or surf on dunes of blazing sand—striving to bring sport into surreal environments. A volcano boarding event in Nicaragua measured heart rates skyrocketing, adrenaline at peak. The danger is immense, the thrill immeasurable. It's humanity's stubbornness in challenging even Earth's fiercest terrains. The result? Pure astonishment. If we can turn searing lava fields into a playground, what can't we conquer? Suddenly, we realize the human drive for sport is limitless, and we can only exclaim: Wow, never would I have imagined such a thing!

Chapter 8:
Mind Illusions and Psychological Curiosities

The Schrödinger's cat paradox and multiple perceptions in our minds

The famous Schrödinger's cat, suspended between life and death until the box is opened, is a quantum metaphor that also reflects how the human mind can hold multiple interpretations of the same event. Before we focus on a detail, the brain entertains different versions of reality. Only when we pay attention does perception settle on a single interpretation, like deciding if the cat is alive or dead. This suggests that our experience of the world is not an objective snapshot but a dynamic process where the mind chooses which reality to "see."

An Aroma That Unlocks Ancient Memories

A single scent can revive childhood memories thought lost decades ago. Scientists know that smell is the sense most directly linked to emotional memory. Experiments show that the aroma of freshly baked cookies can recall a grandmother's kitchen with greater vividness than any photograph. Smells are keys that open memory's locked doors, reminding us that the brain is not a dusty archive but an emotional landscape waiting to be explored by our noses.

The Glitch in Our Mental Timeline

Many people encounter a situation that feels uncannily familiar even though it's new. This mysterious déjà vu is a short-circuit between perception and memory. Researchers suggest minor timing errors or misfiled recollections create this odd sensation. One survey found that around 60% of people have experienced this false sense of having "already lived" a moment. Like a glitch in the matrix, déjà vu shows that our perception of time and experience is not flawless but a flexible puzzle our minds continuously piece together.

The Trickery Behind Your Eyes

Some lines look longer than they are, hollow faces appear in relief, or static images seem to move. Optical illusions like Müller-Lyer or the hollow-face effect prove that vision is not a mere camera lens. The brain interprets, corrects, simplifies, and sometimes deceives itself. One research center noted that over 80% of viewers fall for the same visual trick. Facing these images is like watching a magic show inside our heads. We know there is a trick, yet we cannot help but fall for it again and again.

The Mind's Quest for Patterns

Humans dislike randomness and try to link events even where no link exists. This is how superstitions and irrational beliefs emerge, from black cats "bringing" bad luck to elaborate rituals to "ensure" victory. A poll shows that more than 70% of people admit at least one small superstition. It's the brain's strategy to impose patterns and meaning on uncertainty. Even if these correlations are unreal, the mind accepts them as anchors of stability in a stormy sea of chance.

Colors and Flavors

Identical beverages, one transparent and one dyed red, lead most tasters to consider the red one sweeter. A test recorded a 30% difference in judgments despite the drinks being the same. This proves that sight and taste interact, and our final perception emerges from this collaboration. The brain does not process inputs in isolation. It blends them, sometimes distorting reality. It's as if our eyes add invisible sugar, revealing that our senses never work in sealed compartments.

When Senses Collide

Some individuals see colors when they hear music or taste flavors when reading words. This condition, synesthesia, is not a defect but a different way of wiring sensory pathways. Neurological studies identify various forms of synesthesia, some extremely rare. A synesthete might describe a violin as "mint green" or the number five as "electric blue." It's a glimpse into the diversity of human perception, reminding us that what we call normal is merely a statistical average, not a universal rule.

The Contagious Power of a Smile

A smile is one of the most universally recognizable nonverbal cues, and it's contagious. Seeing someone smile activates similar facial muscles in the observer. An international study found that 50% of people, upon seeing a smile, respond by smiling back spontaneously. It's a form of empathic mirroring, evidence of our social nature. In a world of different languages, the smile remains a code anyone can understand, a social glue proving that the brain is wired for harmony with others.

Music That Shapes Our Sense of Time

A slow piece of music can make minutes feel stretched, while a fast rhythm can make them seem to race by. In one experiment, people exposed to upbeat tunes overestimated the elapsed time by about 20%. The brain uses rhythm as an internal metronome. This flexibility in temporal perception is a quiet everyday magic. We do not control the clock, but the mind manipulates it, gifting us with subjective experiences of duration.

Order in Our Surroundings and Mood Changes

A tidy space, with objects neatly aligned, can relax us. A messy environment can unsettle or annoy. Experiments show that people viewing images of orderly rooms report feelings of calm, while messy scenes raise discomfort. The mind responds to spatial composition like it does to a musical score. Order feels like harmonious melody, chaos a discordant note. This reveals how even small details in the environment shape our mental well-being.

The Placebo Effect

Believing in an effective treatment can alleviate symptoms even if the pill is just sugar. The placebo effect has puzzled researchers for decades, showing how mental conviction can modulate pain or discomfort. A clinical trial recorded improvements in about 30% of patients on placebo. It's not magic but the brain's pharmacy at work, producing real physiological responses. This phenomenon amazes us: if the mind can influence the body's sensations, then perception and belief become powerful allies in feeling better.

Strange Phobias

Some people fear umbrellas or fruits. These bizarre phobias demonstrate how the mind can link anxiety and terror to neutral objects. Lists of unusual phobias, like fear of clowns (coulrophobia) or rubber ducks, show that logic is not the mind's only guide. Any object can turn into a symbol of threat if the brain forms negative associations. It's a testament to how strongly emotions can bend our internal maps of the world.

Cognitive Biases

The mind uses shortcuts that lead us astray. Confirmation bias makes us seek only what aligns with our beliefs, while anchoring effect ties judgments to an initial arbitrary number. Psychologists have identified dozens of such mental pitfalls. Their existence is startling: we are not perfect calculators, but beings who negotiate reality through subjective filters. Knowing about biases makes us wary, reminding us that rationality is not always at the helm.

Finding Faces Everywhere

We find faces in clouds, electrical outlets, random textures. Pareidolia reveals how the brain is a face-detecting machine. Surveys show that 85% of people recall at least once spotting a human visage in inanimate objects. This trait underscores the importance of face recognition for our species, so vital that we see faces where they do not exist. It's a charming quirk of an oversocial mind.

False Memories

It is possible to "implant" memories that never happened through subtle suggestions. A study found that after certain questions, 30% of participants "remembered" a fictional event. The brain is not a flawless video recorder. It reconstructs, edits, modifies. A single hint can sprout a false recollection. This fact unsettles us: if we cannot fully trust our memories, how much of our personal history is a story spun by the mind?

Brilliant Ideas Under the Shower

Many brilliant insights appear while relaxing under a shower. Science suggests that when we are not focused on a problem, the mind wanders and finds unexpected connections. A test showed that distracted individuals had a 20% higher chance of discovering creative solutions. As if the unconscious toils behind the scenes. The warm water, the private setting favor the emergence of fresh thoughts. It reminds us that creativity loves breaks and playful pauses.

Color Coding and Traffic Signs

Red means danger or stop, green means go, yellow means caution. These associations are cultural but deeply ingrained. Tests show that people react 30% faster to a red stop sign than to a neutral color. The brain responds to colors like to emotional signals, used in signage for quick instructions. Each traffic light is a chromatic dialogue with the mind, a silent language that taps into primal reactions.

Lucid Dreams

In lucid dreams, you know you are dreaming and can alter the dream's storyline. Rare but well-documented, this phenomenon shows that consciousness is not a single state. Some dreamers report flying, shifting scenes, meeting imaginary characters by willpower. It's a surprise that our awareness can light up inside a dream, an elastic stretch of reality proving that the mind's frontiers extend even into sleep's domain.

The Brain Filling in What's Not There

Unfinished sentences, incomplete images, open-ended plots: the mind hates gaps and infers meanings. Tests on broken shapes show most people perceive them as complete forms. The brain is a creative force that interprets fragments, adding coherence where none exists. This capacity highlights our active role in constructing the world we experience, not mere observers but co-authors of our perceived reality.

The Universe in a Blot

Rorschach inkblots show ambiguous shapes, and the mind "sees" animals, faces, or surreal landscapes. Despite debates on clinical value, these tests reveal how we project interpretations onto vagueness. Like gazing at clouds and spotting dragons, we impose patterns on the shapeless. The mind refuses emptiness, weaving sense from nothing. These inkblots leave us with a final "wow": if we can find universes in a random blot of ink, what can't imagination achieve?

Chapter 9:
Travels Traditions and Unusual Geographies

Tiny Nations, Big Stories

Some countries are so small they make a big-city district look large. San Marino, with about 34,000 inhabitants and its three towers on Mount Titano, or Liechtenstein, covering just over 160 km², show that a nation doesn't depend on sheer size. There are even microstates with only a few hundred citizens, almost an extended family with their own flag and government. A researcher counted over a dozen of these geopolitical curiosities, where international politics unfold in areas smaller than a golf course. A reminder that sovereignty can emerge even from a piece of land no bigger than a postage stamp.

A Desert That Turns Into a Colorful Garden of Flowers

If you think a desert is unchangeably barren, think again. In Chile's Atacama Desert, after a rare rainfall, hundreds of vibrant flowers bloom within days. Botanists have recorded up to 200 species appearing suddenly, attracting astonished visitors. This fleeting spectacle overturns the image of a monotonous landscape, revealing hidden potential under the sand. An unexpected surprise for anyone convinced that nothing could ever blossom in such a place.

The Wandering Islands

Not all islands are fixed in place. Some sand and debris formations, propelled by currents and tides, appear, vanish, or migrate within months. In the Pacific, observers saw an "ephemeral island" emerge in 2017 and vanish by 2019. A geographer describes mobile islets on the Amazon River, shifting local maps each season. It's as if geography is playing a hidden card game, disproving the idea of an unchanging Earth. Discovering that even an island can "migrate" reveals a planet in constant flux.

Sunken Cities, Living Memories

Ruins of ancient civilizations lie beneath the waves. In the Mediterranean or near Japan, temples, ports, and statues rest underwater. Marine archaeologists have cataloged columns and mosaics on the seabed, remnants of vanished peoples. These lost cities, accessible only with diving gear, blend history with marine biology. Imagining once-bustling streets now inhabited by curious fish suggests a second life where the past sinks into the ocean's embrace, awaiting rediscovery.

Borders of Identity

Some areas have aspired to autonomy or secession for generations. Cultural identities run deep, challenging official borders. An anthropologist counted at least 50 active independence movements, some centuries old. Here, language, traditions, and belonging surpass political lines drawn on maps. This tension reminds us that boundaries aren't eternal lines but historical compromises subject to negotiation. Every map can mirror passions and unrealized dreams.

Love's Quirky Traditions

Not all newlyweds settle for rings and bouquets. In certain villages, couples must overcome bizarre trials or exchange eccentric gifts—like dried fish or outlandish symbolic objects—to seal their union. An ethnographer describes ceremonies where relatives stage mini athletic contests to "earn" the wedding feast. Marriage becomes a showcase of creativity and tradition, far beyond simple formality, making us smile and ponder the variety of roads leading to love.

Tea Rituals Beyond Expectations

Not only Japan or China: in remote regions, tea takes on different roles. In some highland areas of Central Asia, rare herbs are mixed in for healing properties; in parts of Africa, tea may serve as a sacred act or a link to ancestors. A researcher found dozens of unknown customs, proving that tea is a cultural code with countless variations. What's a daily beverage in one place becomes a mysterious ceremony elsewhere.

Villages Where the Official Language Doesn't Exist

In certain isolated spots, despite being within a country with a recognized national tongue, locals speak ancient dialects or minority languages unknown to outsiders. A linguist discovered communities where nobody understands the official language, as if living in a time capsule. These linguistic enclaves show that verbal boundaries ignore political borders, tracing invisible lines of sound and memory— linguistic puzzles hidden from the mainstream.

Monuments Concealed in Dense Jungles

Temples, giant statues, and megalithic structures lie hidden in the heart of impenetrable forests. Only modern technology—drones and satellite images—has revealed archaeological treasures overlooked for centuries. An archaeologist recounts an Amazonian sanctuary spotted from the air. These discoveries rewrite history, adding unforeseen pieces to our past's puzzle, reminding us that nature can hide incredible secrets beneath a cloak of green silence.

Lanterns of Light and Hope

During certain festivals, thousands of glowing lanterns are placed on rivers or lakes, creating a fairy-tale scene reflected on the water's surface. Participants send their wishes, thanks, and memories adrift with the lights. An anthropologist observed people watching in silence, mesmerized by these small floating beacons like traveling dreams. It's a silent choreography of hope skimming across liquid mirrors—a collective trust in the beauty of the ephemeral.

Sports and Dances of Remote Islands

On tiny, isolated islands off the tourist trail, ancient games and dances pass from generation to generation. An ethnographer documented dances imitating local seabirds or sports using natural materials, reflecting the environment's influence. These expressions go beyond entertainment: they're living chapters of collective memory, a bond between human life, nature, and ancestors.

Sacred Places Off-Limits to Most

Some sacred places remain forbidden to the masses. Shrines hidden in caves, altars on distant mountains—accessible only to a few initiates. Their inaccessibility intensifies the aura of mystery. An anthropologist tells of a Tibetan sanctuary visible from afar yet off-limits to outsiders. Here, geography becomes a metaphor: a boundary between what can be known and what remains a sacred enigma.

Inverted Maps

Who decided north must be at the top? There are maps with south on top or projections that warp continents in puzzling ways. A collector shows ancient charts where Europe sits at the bottom. Such visuals prove that orientation and geographic conventions are not absolute. Changing perspective reveals that a map is no objective truth but a narrative of power, history, and cultural choice.

Rainbow Mountains

Some places feature geological layers producing vibrant stripes on hills and mountains, from fiery reds to bright yellows. These "rainbow mountains" in Peru or China leave visitors feeling small before natural artistry. A geologist notes mineral deposits create these hues. This surreal landscape denies the gray monotony of common rock, offering a chromatic spectacle that feels like discovering a secret painter working underground.

Cities with Unusual Urban Geometry

Not all plazas are square. Some towns boast circular squares or bizarre street plans. An urban planner studied a village with a perfectly round plaza, an inheritance from religious or symbolic traditions. Such unexpected shapes reflect cultural motives. Each city can have its geometric secrets—architectural stories told through curves and angles, reminding us that urban planning can break free from conventional lines.

Forgotten Pilgrimage Routes Through Silent Forests

Ancient spiritual paths once thronged by pilgrims now lie nearly vanished beneath roots and undergrowth. A researcher uncovered maps of old sacred trails, barely known today, yet still laden with meaning. Walking these hidden routes, imagining monks and travelers from centuries past, becomes a journey into a spiritual dimension of geography. The silence of the woods holds echoes of old prayers waiting for anyone who cares to listen.

The Bridge Linking Two Continents

Some infrastructures, like Istanbul's Bosphorus Bridge, physically connect two continents. Crossing that asphalt ribbon takes you from Europe to Asia in minutes. It's not just engineering; it's a symbol of cultures meeting, challenging the idea that continents or natural divides must be insurmountable barriers. This bridge becomes a metaphor for contact, a reminder that lines on a map are not always walls but sometimes gateways.

Harvest Festivals with Eerie Masks

In some rural celebrations, harvest time involves frightening masks and odd costumes to scare away evil spirits or summon fertility. An ethnographer details rites where participants paint their faces with pigments and play mythic roles in the fields. These events transform agriculture into metaphorical theater, blending human, land, and myth into a vivid and symbolic performance. A proof that working the earth can also mean working the imagination.

Floating Markets and Amphibious Cultures

In certain places, markets float on canals or lagoons, with boats as shops and water as roads. Life flows along liquid streets, trade adapting to aquatic logic. An anthropologist describes a Thai floating market where bargaining moves at the pace of gentle currents. It's a microcosm where waterways replace sidewalks and where human adaptation crafts a lifestyle balanced between land and water.

Calendars That Don't Recognize 365 Days

Not everyone follows the Gregorian calendar. In Ethiopia, the year has thirteen months; other systems count seasons differently. A chronology expert identified a dozen active temporal systems. This reminds us that time, like space, is culturally constructed. Imagining a world where a year is longer or divided differently forces us to rethink our references, realizing how our measure of hours and days reflects human minds, not the stars.

Chapter 10:
Technology Gadgets and Bizarre Inventions

The First Wearable Computer

Decades ago, long before we had smartwatches and fitness trackers, a few researchers tinkered with bulky "wearable" computers strapped to the body, complete with dangling cables and battery packs in pockets. They looked like something out of a low-budget sci-fi movie, yet they were the pioneers of wearable tech. Today, fitness bands and smartwatches feel normal, but back then these contraptions drew puzzled stares. They were the first attempts to free computers from desks, anticipating by decades the wearable revolution we now take for granted.

Robotic Chefs

Not just mechanical arms for assembly lines—some prototypes of kitchen robots can cook complex recipes, measuring ingredients to the milligram. Imagine a machine following instructions from a Michelin-starred chef, chopping, blending, and plating dishes without a stray crumb. One London-based startup tested a "robotic cook" that can produce a gourmet meal indistinguishable from a human chef's creation. The scenario suggests a future where kitchens host culinary androids, blending coded precision with gastronomic artistry.

Gadgets for Ironing Clothes on the Go

No need to hunt down a hotel iron. Some quirky inventions aim to smooth wrinkles out of clothes while you're traveling or even walking around. Heated hangers, portable presses, and odd contraptions promise to eliminate creases on shirts and trousers in motion. A camping accessory company proposed a heated hook for the travel closet. While not a primary need, these gadgets show that technology tries to address even the tiniest annoyances—like stubborn wrinkles—offering unusual solutions to everyday problems.

Drones Delivering Plush Toys Just for Fun

Not only drones for urgent medicines or packages. Some experiments involve drones carrying small, utterly useless items like teddy bears. A researcher once orchestrated the air-drop of stuffed animals to surprise onlookers below. Perhaps pointless, but it reminds us that technology need not always be serious or goal-oriented. Sometimes it's just a playful stunt to make people chuckle, proving we can also enjoy a frivolous side of innovation.

Typewriters Sending Emails

There are artisanal projects connecting old mechanical typewriters to the internet, turning them into keyboards for sending emails. Every keystroke makes a satisfying metallic click, while letters appear digitally on-screen or travel through cyberspace. It's a marriage of eras: the solid charm of a vintage device and the fluidity of instant communication. A nostalgic bridge between the smell of ink and the speed of email.

A 3D-Printed Spare Wheel on Demand

3D printing isn't just for design prototypes anymore. Today we can print spare parts—like a bike's extra wheel—right at home. One startup makes reinforced plastic filaments for durable components. No more waiting at a store: with the correct file, you print what you need in a matter of hours. A revolution in logistics, an infinite virtual catalog of replacements ready to take shape on your desk.

Elevators Without Cables

Imagine elevators that move not only up and down, but also sideways, using magnetic levitation or other cable-free solutions. Such prototypes redefine how we think of skyscrapers, turning buildings into three-dimensional mazes where the cabin travels like a subway car among floors and corridors. The idea of an elevator "freed" from gravity's usual constraints feels like sci-fi, opening doors to fluid, multi-directional architecture.

Cars Changing Color at the Push of a Button

Electrochromic paints allow a car to shift its hue with a simple electric current. One day you might leave home with a gray car and return in bright blue. This concept, tested in automotive design labs, suggests that vehicle customization could become instantaneous, like choosing an outfit each morning. A playful vision of personal style extended to your car's exterior.

Devices That Translate Thoughts into Text

Brain-computer interfaces (BCIs) are starting to decode neural signals and turn them into written words. Though still slow and complex, they hint at new communication methods for people who can't speak or move. It's not telepathy, but interpreting brainwaves into language is a scenario that could revolutionize how our minds and machines connect—an evolutionary step toward blending thought and technology.

Houses Built in a Day

Giant 3D printers can now extrude special cement to build walls and entire house structures in mere hours. This is no longer sci-fi: some cities are testing rapid construction sites that cut costs and time drastically. Engineers talk about reducing days to hours, making building more like manufacturing, with fewer wastes and more efficiency. A radical shift in how we shape our living spaces.

A Pen That Draws in Mid-Air

Special pens heat plastic filaments so you can "draw" objects in thin air. Not limited to paper, artists create small sculptures from nothing, instantly giving form to ideas. One designer crafted miniature figurines and flowers suspended mid-air. It's drawing turned into instant sculpting, letting creativity break free from flat surfaces.

Objects That Repair Themselves

Some paints or plastics contain microscopic resin capsules. If scratched, the capsules break and fill the damage, mending the surface like skin healing a wound. This "self-repair" concept extends an object's life, cutting maintenance and waste. A step toward more durable, self-sustaining items—like having built-in healing for our belongings.

DNA-Based Computers

Instead of silicon chips, some scientists are exploring computations using DNA molecules. These "biological computers" leverage chemical reactions to solve problems. It's an entirely new model, blending informatics with biology and potentially reshaping speed and efficiency. A paradigm shift where hardware isn't plastic and metal, but organic matter, hinting at an unprecedented alliance of science and nature.

Tuning the Atmosphere to Your Mood

LED smart bulbs adjust color and brightness, syncing with time of day or personal preferences. This means lighting can be tailored to relax you at night or energize you in the morning. Not just a simple on/off switch, but a light director shaping your indoor well-being. Technology enters domestic life more intimately, guiding emotions with subtle illumination.

Holographic Films

Holographic films on glass can project landscapes, information, or graphics. Your window becomes an interactive display. One day you might wake up to see weather reports or a virtual forest on your pane. It's a blend of interior design and augmented reality, merging comfort and digital enhancement into everyday views.

Transparent Solar Panels

Researchers are developing translucent solar panels integrated into windows, capturing specific wavelengths of light. Your window could generate electricity without blocking the view. Elegance, sustainability, and function unite, turning buildings into subtle power sources. It's no longer enough to let in the sun; now we can store its energy silently.

Anti-Gravity Backpacks

Prototypes of backpacks with suspension systems reduce impact on your back as you walk, making the load feel lighter. One company tested a model absorbing up to 30% of the shock. It's a step toward less tiring hikes, blending biomechanics and ergonomics, hinting at a near-futuristic ease in carrying our essentials.

Shoes with Integrated GPS

Footwear with built-in vibrations can guide you through unfamiliar cities. A gentle buzz on the left foot means turn left, on the right foot means turn right. No more staring at a phone map—just follow your feet. A discreet technology guiding your steps in the real world, merging navigation and comfort seamlessly.

Glasses That Brew Coffee?

Some designers imagine utterly useless concepts—like glasses warming water for instant espresso, or hats baking cookies. Although no practical use exists yet, these show how creativity can push beyond the reasonable, turning the bizarre into a testbed for future invention. The human mind explores even ridiculous paths, possibly inspiring tomorrow's breakthrough.

A Singing Fridge

Smart fridges that play sounds, music, or voice alerts when opened exist to add a hint of entertainment to domestic life. It's not essential, but it brings a smile. Home automation isn't just about efficiency and control, it can also amuse, making technology not only useful but fun. A reminder not to take the digital world too seriously.

Share Your Experience

Did you know that, according to some studies, most readers rely on the comments of those who've already flipped through the pages before deciding to pick up a book? Every review—whether enthusiastic or more critical—can really make a difference for those who follow in your footsteps. I'll personally read your feedback to understand what resonates, what entertains, and what might be improved. Think of your review as a fellow traveler's tip, an honest guide for other explorers of curiosity. If you have a moment, would you leave your mark? Thanks for your contribution—just a few words can help light the way for those who come next.

Scan to leave a review on Amazon if you live in the US

Scan to leave a review on Amazon if you live in the UK

Scan to leave a review on Amazon if you live in Canada

Scan to leave a review on Amazon if you live in Australia

Chapter 11:
Myths, Folklore & Imaginary Creatures

The Dragon Slumbering Beneath Ancient Mountains

Have you ever imagined that beneath a nearby mountain range a colossal dragon might be sleeping? In many traditions, mighty winged creatures rest in the earth's depths, silent for centuries. Some say that in times of crisis or when nature's balance falters, these dragons awaken, emerging from stone and minerals with a roar that shakes the valleys. Across different cultures, the dragon beneath the mountain stands as a symbol of primordial strength and ancient wisdom, a reminder that the planet's hidden power can stir at any moment, shaking off ages of stillness.

Mischievous Woodland Fairies in the Northern Forests

Picture yourself strolling through a Scandinavian woodland at dusk. You sense a faint giggle, a rustle that's not just the wind. According to old Celtic and Nordic tales, tiny, mischievous fairies thrive among moss and ferns, delighting in tricks to confuse travelers—tying blades of grass into knots, swapping stones to lead wanderers astray. They're not evil, but playful guardians of the wild, a gentle warning that nature's green world is never fully tamed. Encountering them means accepting that you might lose your way, smiling as you discover the forest's secret humor.

Feathered Serpents of Mesoamerica

Have you ever heard of serpents adorned with bright feathers and divine powers? In pre-Columbian legends, beings like Quetzalcóatl combine reptilian strength with airy grace. They are no mere animals, but deities of creation, spiritual guides, and fertility symbols. These creatures taught agriculture, marked astronomical cycles, and linked the heavens to the soil. For Mesoamerican peoples, the feathered serpent was a cosmic force uniting the natural world and the stars, showing that nature's boundaries can blur, and divine creativity can nest in unexpected forms.

The Celtic Water Horse

Envision a misty coastline in Western Europe. On the shore stands a magnificent horse, its mane damp with seawater, beckoning passersby to ride. But beware: this maritime steed comes from legends where once mounted, it plunges into the depths, never returning. A lesson woven into Celtic stories, it warns against naive trust in mysterious wonders. The water horse is a metaphor for the perils of the unknown, reminding us that what glimmers at the boundary between land and ocean may lure us to unfathomable abysses.

The American Mothman

In American lore, some claim to have glimpsed a humanoid figure with moth-like wings and glowing red eyes. Known as the Mothman, it's said to appear in tense times or before disasters, feeding urban folklore and modern cryptozoology. Perhaps just collective illusion, optical trickery, or ancient fears rekindled. Real or not, the Mothman reveals that human imagination needs no primeval forest to birth monsters. Even amid neon-lit streets and highways, a mysterious silhouette can embody the city's modern anxieties and uncertainties.

Ghostly Lights in Desert Nights

In certain desert regions, people speak of strange will-o'-the-wisps or drifting lights appearing at twilight. Tiny luminous orbs flicker on the horizon, vanishing if approached. Locals interpret them as wandering souls, restless spirits, or otherworldly presences. While science suggests gases or electrical phenomena, legends endure. Where explanations falter, fascination thrives. In the silent emptiness of the desert, even a faint glimmer can become a window into the unexplained, a brief glow defying the barren monotony.

The Latin American Chupacabra

Have you heard of the chupacabra, the "goat-sucker" haunting pastures in Latin America? Stories say it attacks livestock, leaving strange bite marks and drained carcasses. Perhaps born from misidentified animals and fueled by sensational reports, the chupacabra reflects a collective dread of unknown predators in the darkness. Existence aside, the tale persists, a shadowy figure where fear and curiosity meet. It's a reminder that humanity craves the thrill of a lurking monster, even if it prowls only in whispered midnight tales.

The Golem's Eternal Lesson

In Jewish folklore, the golem is a silent giant of clay or mud, brought to life by sacred words. A tireless guardian and warning sign, it challenges the idea of humans playing divine creators. The golem's presence raises moral questions: giving life without responsibility can backfire. Though ancient, this dilemma resonates today, in labs and workshops shaping robots and AI. The old myth echoes in modern times, hinting that our ambitions must be balanced by humility.

Marine Demons and Krakens in Northern Sagas

In northern seas, sailors speak of krakens, colossal squid-like beasts capable of sinking whole ships, and monstrous serpents lurking in icy depths. Such stories emerged from awe and terror at an endless ocean. The kraken is the symbol of the uncontrollable, reminding us that the world's vast waters laugh at human attempts to dominate them. Even as navigation charts improve, these marine myths survive, ensuring we never forget how small we are before the boundless blue.

The Deer-Woman

In certain Asian tales, a woman can take an animal form—a deer, perhaps—bridging human and wild domains. This shape-shifting reflects cultures that see no absolute line between man and beast. The deer-woman stands for a cosmos where identities mingle, and nature's rhythms flow through our veins. She's an invitation to appreciate life's fluidity, understanding that our roots extend into forests, streams, and the silent steps of a graceful creature at dusk.

Lamassu of Mesopotami

In ancient Mesopotamia, statues of lamassu watched over palaces: bodies of bulls, eagle wings, human heads. They fused strength, wisdom, and divinity. Each lamassu was a living mosaic of virtues, carved in stone to inspire awe and trust. These beings symbolized unity in diversity, reminding viewers that no single element suffices alone. A testament to a time when art and myth intertwined, warning and comforting, asserting that might and intellect must walk hand in hand.

Sirens and the Irresistible Call of Ruin

The sirens' song, famous since the Odyssey, is a melody so enchanting it lures sailors onto deadly rocks. Found in countless maritime legends, these half-women, half-creatures warn us that beauty can mask danger. Their voices are honeyed traps punishing hubris and gullibility. Like a timeless cautionary tale, the siren reminds us that what sounds delightful may hide disaster, and that wisdom lies in recognizing when to plug our ears against the most seductive tunes.

Werewolves and the Beast Within Man

On nights of a full moon, a man may turn into a wolf, unleashing primal fury and appetite. Werewolf myths surface worldwide, suggesting that beneath our civilized veneer lurks an ancient animality. These stories speak of fear and fascination with losing control, revealing the uneasy tension between reason and primal instinct. The wolf-man warns that no matter how we refine ourselves, the wilderness of our own hearts might break free.

Vampires Beyond Europe

Not just Dracula and Carpathian castles. Vampiric beings appear in Africa, Asia, and the islands of distant oceans. Creatures of the night feed on blood or life force, a universal fear that crosses borders. Each culture customizes these nocturnal predators to reflect its own anxieties about death, disease, and moral transgression. Vampires, whether elegant or monstrous, stand as a global sign that fear of the dark and its unknown dwellers is shared by humanity everywhere.

Talking Trees in African Lore

In certain African traditions, trees can speak, offering counsel or punishing wrongdoing. They are not passive wood but living witnesses of centuries, imbued with memory and spirit. These legends treat forests as halls of elders, where whispering leaves carry advice. The talking tree reminds us that nature can be teacher, judge, and friend—if we learn to listen. A spiritual bond that encourages reverence for the green world.

Lake Monsters

Not only Loch Ness in Scotland claims a mysterious monster. Lakes in Africa, Asia, and the Americas host their own elusive beings, fueling local tales. Whether or not these creatures exist, the legends spark tourism, curiosity, and a touch of hope that something mysterious lurks beneath the surface. They don't need scientific proof to thrive: a whispered rumor, an old photo, and people keep peering into the water, dreaming of shadows that defy explanation.

The Himalayan Yeti

In Himalayan heights, the yeti, or "abominable snowman," is said to roam unseen. Whether mistaken bears or illusions, the myth persists.

Why does the yeti fascinate us? Perhaps it represents that final frontier not yet tamed by civilization. With satellites mapping every corner, the yeti stands for the faint possibility that nature holds surprises beyond our charts. A comforting thought: the world still has room for the unknowable.

Mischievous Teachers of Hidden Truths

Figures like Loki, Coyote, or Anansi disrupt order, playing pranks on gods and humans alike. They bend rules, sow confusion, and force reflection on moral values through laughter and chaos. Tricksters aren't evil; they're mirrors and jesters, showing that not everything is black and white. Their antics remind us that life's lessons can emerge from clever deceptions and that humility often grows after a well-spun trick.

The Evolution of the Mythical Unicorn

Unicorns may have originated from travelers' flawed reports of exotic animals like rhinoceroses. But medieval Europe turned the unicorn into a symbol of purity and spiritual grace, its horn rumored to cleanse poison and evil. Over time, this beast evolved from cryptid to cultural icon, proving how imagination reshapes meaning. The unicorn's story is a journey from natural anomaly to exalted emblem of innocence, a tribute to the human capacity for transforming the unknown into shining ideals.

The Phoenix and the Promise of Rebirth from Fire

The phoenix, a bird consumed by flames only to rise again from its ashes, appears in many cultures as a sign of hope. It assures us that after every ending, a new beginning awaits. Amid cycles of life and death, the phoenix stands for resilience and renewal. Its fiery resurrection whispers that no defeat is final, no darkness without eventual dawn. A universal metaphor of overcoming adversity, encouraging us to trust that even after destruction, something beautiful can be born anew.

Chapter 12:
Pop Culture & Absurd Trends

Viral Fads Born Out of Nowhere

Ever think a random video shot in your living room could spark a global phenomenon? Statistics show that about 70% of explosive trends arise with zero planning. A girl in pajamas dances on camera, a bizarre meme emerges from a hidden forum, and within a week millions imitate those moves, share that image, or repeat that catchphrase without knowing its source. It's like a tiny spark that, instead of dying, sets the entire media forest aflame. Virality is the unexpected made powerful: one moment you're a nobody, the next you're at the heart of a worldwide ritual, all because someone halfway across the globe hit "share."

Popular Dances on Social Media

Have you ever wondered how many people learned dance steps from a clip only a few seconds long? One study reveals 55% of social users tried at least once to mimic a choreography they saw online. From the most delirious "challenges" to simple, elegant moves, these dances unite grandparents and teenagers, executives and students. It's as if the world has become one huge digital dance floor where everyone tries to keep in step. In 2019, one runaway hit song got people dancing in over 90 countries—an actual rhythmic group hug across the planet. Think about it: a borderless party, a virtual rave making our feet tap in sync.

Collectible Gadgets Inspired by TV Shows

Ever wanted a figurine of a minor TV character known only to a handful of fans? Now you can. Action figures of background roles, mugs emblazoned with obscure quotes, exact replicas of iconic props—merchandising digs deep into fictional worlds, looking for Easter eggs to turn into tangible treasures. In 2021, a pillow resembling a hat from a character who appeared for only ten seconds in one episode sold for $500. Owning a physical piece of that universe means anchoring fantasy to reality. The obsession proves pop culture can materialize, conquering shelves with the same intensity it conquers hearts.

Music Festivals in the Most Unlikely Places

Why stick to a stadium or a concert hall? Today's festivals pop up on mountaintops at 3,000 meters, in the heart of the desert, or even floating on a lake. Organizers choose wild backdrops to deliver unique experiences, where sound meets breathtaking scenery. In 2018, an event in the Sahara drew 2,000 intrepid souls eager to say, "I was there." These unusual venues show pop culture's hunger for fresh emotions: not content with a simple stage, it craves adventure, the story you'll proudly tell friends.

Carnival Costumes Inspired by Memes

No more generic pirates or princesses: now people hit the streets dressed as the latest viral meme. Wearing a costume that embodies the "Doge" dog or recreating the "Harlem Shake" dance in fabric form means dragging online humor into the physical world of confetti and laughter. In 2020, a major European carnival saw that 15% of costumes referenced internet memes. It's the digital inside joke stepping off the screen and parading through real life. Memes become flesh and fabric, pop culture remixing itself in a thousand shapes.

Food Branded by Pop Stars and Influencers

Who would have imagined that snacks bearing an influencer's name could sell out in hours? Or ice creams endorsed by a pop star doubling a gelateria's sales just with a tweet? In 2019, a chocolate tied to a famous YouTuber sold out in 48 hours. The idea of "tasting" a celebrity is astounding: fame no longer just hits our ears or eyes, it tickles our taste buds. It's like a marketing dessert trolley, where pop culture flavors can literally be consumed, a metaphor for how media power infiltrates every sense.

Why Redo Everything?

Films from the '80s remade with modern effects, classic TV series rebooted, vintage games revived for next-gen consoles—remakes feed on nostalgia. Statistics show that 80% of remakes at least pique initial public curiosity. Yet not everyone's pleased: some sigh, wondering where originality went. Perhaps it's a collective ritual: revisiting the past comforts us, like opening an old photo album. A cocktail of melancholy and convenience, a merchandised déjà vu that might one day make us say, "I never thought they'd do it again."

Pop Stars Without Bodies

No need for a human vocalist or flesh-and-blood charisma. Digital icons like Hatsune Miku gather fan clubs, hold holographic concerts, sell merch. Celebrity can now be software, fan passion pouring into pixels. It's pop culture's new frontier: fame detached from physical form, proving that a star can be a pure data construct. The spotlight no longer needs a human face—just a cleverly programmed avatar.

Odd Museums Devoted to Celebrities

Not just wax figures, but entire museums dedicated to a single actor or singer's most banal possessions. Cups, napkins, even old receipts become relics because a star once touched them. In Japan, a fan-run "hall of relics" holds over 3,000 items linked to one famous actor. It's the ecstasy of fandom, where ordinary objects gain sacred aura. A testament that pop culture can sanctify the trivial, turning every crumb of celebrity life into an exhibit worthy of a ticket.

Themed Restaurants Paying Homage to Cult Films

Imagine entering a diner and feeling like you've stepped onto a movie set. Waiters dressed as characters, menu items named after famous quotes, decor that replicates iconic scenes. Eating here is more than a meal; it's a narrative experience. Cinephiles enjoy a menu that recalls beloved storylines, merging culinary pleasure with cinematic nostalgia. Pop culture invades the kitchen, making lunch a mini-episode of your favorite saga.

Movie Props Sold at Absurd Prices

At auction, an object seen for mere seconds in a blockbuster can fetch thousands. In 2020, a pair of glasses worn by a minor role reached sky-high bids. Why pay so much? Because it's not just a hat or a mug, it's a spark of magic, a tangible shard of that film's universe. This phenomenon shows how storytelling inflates value: the aura of a narrative can make everyday things priceless treasures, proving that pop culture can generate gold from dust.

Cartoons Turned into Fashion Legends

Cartoon characters from childhood appear on haute couture runways. In 2019, about 20% of surveyed designers admitted using cartoon imagery for inspiration. The irony and whimsy of cartoons meet the elegance of tailoring. It's a fusion where simple graphics meet refined fabrics, proving that pop culture can spark a smile in even the most exclusive circles. Nostalgia and style dance hand in hand, lighting up the catwalk with animated flair.

Secret Cameos by Directors in Their Films

Some directors sneak themselves into their works as hidden extras. It's a visual Easter egg rewarding sharp-eyed fans. Hitchcock did it often, and many followed. This playful wink forges a bond, as viewers feel included in a private joke. Spotting the cameo is like finding a secret signature, turning watching a movie into a treasure hunt, a moment of complicity between creator and audience.

Musical Covers in Invented Languages

Imagine a band covering a hit song with gibberish lyrics. No meaning, just made-up sounds. Audiences laugh, dance, and realize words aren't essential. It's a linguistic experiment proving that pop culture can thrive on pure melody. When sense evaporates, energy and rhythm prevail, reminding us that music can charm with mere phonetics. It's creativity freed from semantics, a joyful sonic puzzle.

Karaoke Fever Taken to the Extreme

Karaoke isn't just friends singing off-key anymore. There are marathon contests lasting 24 hours, record attempts of 48-hour nonstop singing. A communal stage where anyone can be a star for a moment. In some bars, continuous singing sessions transform a simple pastime into a mass phenomenon celebrating the urge to shine, however briefly. Pop culture invites all to taste stardom's sweetness, even if only through a microphone and a random playlist.

Vintage Objects Cycling Back into Style

Vinyl records, Polaroid cameras, arcade machines—every 20 years or so they rise again. In 2022, vinyl sales surpassed CDs for the first time in decades. Nostalgia is a mighty engine, a refuge from digital overload. Pop culture resurrects outdated tech, bridging generations with the charm of imperfection. It's like finding comfort in a familiar old sweater: proving that the past never really dies, it just naps, waiting to be revived in a new cycle of fascination.

Internet Slang That Vanishes in a Blink

Remember that online term everyone used three months ago, now totally forgotten? Web slang is a flash in the pan. Studies show 80% of digital neologisms fade within a year. It's the language of the instant, reflecting our restless era. Each word is a shooting star that burns bright and fast, mirroring how pop culture online is fluid, unstable, and always eager for the next novelty. Yesterday's cool phrase is today's fossil—blink and you miss it.

The World's Strangest Fan Clubs

There are fan communities devoted to the weirdest things: a jingle from an '80s commercial, a minor cartoon character who appeared in two episodes, or the sound effects of old games. Pop culture is a bazaar where any trivial fragment can become an idol. Surveys reveal micro-groups worshipping the most random details, proving that devotion can ignite anywhere. It's the triumph of shared passion over rational choice, a temple of oddities built by collective affection.

Online Fandom Wars

Fans don't just love; they fight. Virtual battles erupt between admirers of rival sagas, bands, or characters. In 2020, a feud between two fantasy fandoms generated millions of comments in a week. It's passion turned combat, a kind of digital soccer match over cultural products. Although it might seem silly, it highlights the emotional force behind pop culture. These flame wars show that people cling fiercely to what they love, treating entertainment like a cause worth defending at all costs.

TV Marathons of Old Forgotten Series

Imagine thousands of viewers streaming a cheesy '70s show labeled mediocre by history. They do it ironically, or to appreciate a certain vintage charm. As they watch outdated effects and stiff acting, they transform mediocrity into collective fun. This is "pop archaeology," celebrating imperfections as hidden gems. A communal experience reminding us that pop culture can find value even in past failures. Who would've guessed that yesterday's trash could unite today's fans in joyful rediscovery? Honestly, who would have thought!

Chapter 13:
Extraordinary Science

Bacteria Discovered by Chance on a Forgotten Sandwich

Picture a weary researcher leaving a half-eaten sandwich in a lab corner and forgetting it for days. When someone finally checks that moldy mess, they find new bacterial species never cataloged before. In 2010, a team at Harvard identified microbes capable of metabolizing unusual compounds in just such a lunch remnant. It's an example of how science can advance through happy accidents. Something as trivial as a neglected snack can open the door to a hidden microbial world, reminding us that sometimes progress arises where nobody would expect it.

Discoveries Born from Flawed Experiments

Did you know that about 30% of major findings in chemistry and biology come from mishaps? Fleming's penicillin is the classic case, but not the only one. In 1945, a chemist's miscalculation led to a super-flexible polymer, a precursor to modern plastics. A 2017 MIT survey confirmed that embracing anomalies is crucial. In research, an error isn't necessarily a failure—it can be a stepping stone to new insights. The secret lies in having eyes keen enough to recognize a lucky slip, like stumbling upon a diamond in a pile of dust.

The Creature That Survives in Open Space

Tardigrades, minuscule organisms less than a millimeter long, withstand deadly conditions: cosmic vacuum, intense radiation, temperature swings from -270°C to over 100°C. In 2007, some were sent into orbit, exposed to space's emptiness, and upon return they "revived" unfazed. It's as if nature created a miniature superhero. A 2019 study showed over 90% endure sterilizing conditions that would kill almost any life form. These "water bears" prove survival can defy known rules, showing us life's resilience is more formidable than any fiction.

Secret Labs Beneath Polar Ice

Thousands of meters under Antarctic ice, scientists extract ice cores dating hundreds of thousands of years back. Each layer traps tiny air bubbles—time capsules of ancient atmospheres. In 2013, a 3,400-meter core revealed insights into climates 800,000 years old, with CO_2 levels much lower than today's. These hidden labs are natural time machines, letting us "read" the planet's climatic past like an old manuscript. Understanding how Earth responded to past cycles of warming and cooling offers clues for the future—no sci-fi needed, just ice and patience.

Brains Preserved to Understand the Human Mind

Some institutions hold collections of human brains in formalin, a macabre yet priceless archive of thousands of specimens. In Denmark, one museum has over 9,000. Studying these tissues helps identify areas linked to complex functions or trace rare neurological diseases. Although it seems eerie, each brain is a neural puzzle offering glimpses into thought and memory. It's a form of "cerebral archaeology," where each sample is a fossil of our inner workings, guiding us to better understand the architecture of the mind.

Monkeys Learning to Use Tablets

Imagine gorillas and orangutans interacting with touchscreens, recognizing shapes and solving digital puzzles. Not sci-fi, but real experiments: in 2015, researchers showed that some capuchin monkeys could recall icon positions on a tablet, associating patterns with rewards. This raises a question: if a primate navigates a simple interface, how far is its mind from ours? The line between human and animal intelligence blurs, suggesting that technological learning may sprout even among forest branches.

Plants That 'Make Music'—Or Something Like It?

No one's expecting a tree strumming a guitar, but experiments show that plants respond to certain sonic vibrations. In 2018, scientists attached sensors to leaves, noticing electrical signal changes with different sounds. Some artistic-scientific projects converted these signals into music-like outputs. While plants aren't consciously playing tunes, their sensitivity to subtle stimuli hints at a more communicative green world than we imagined. Picture a concert in a greenhouse, where plants "participate" silently, broadening our notion of life's responsiveness.

Biological Cryptographers

Storing data in DNA isn't wild speculation—it's reality in experimental phases. In 2017, a team encoded an entire book and a video into DNA strands, retrieving them flawlessly. A single gram of DNA can hold millions of gigabytes, surpassing any hard disk. Companies invest in this technique for ultra-long-term archives. Writing libraries in molecular code blends biology and information technology, transcending conventional memory. It's a new era of data storage, where nature's blueprint doubles as a digital safe.

Particles That Appear and Vanish into Nothing

In the quantum realm, classical logic falters. Virtual particles pop out of the vacuum and disappear in fractions of a second, confirmed by CERN measurements. Imagine bubbles forming and bursting too fast to see, yet influencing fundamental forces. This subatomic stage play reveals a reality more bizarre than any fantasy. The universe's fabric hides ephemeral actors, challenging common sense and showing that what we call "real" is woven from fleeting, invisible performances.

The Mystery of Dark Matter

About 85% of the universe's mass is dark matter: invisible, intangible, but gravitationally influential. Without it, galaxies would fall apart.

Scientists hunt it with underground detectors and space telescopes, but it remains elusive. It's like having a massive, unseen guest in the room. This enigma forces us to reconsider cosmic models, reminding us how little we know. An astronomical question mark fueling our drive to push beyond the known and into the unknown.

Fossils of Bizarre Creatures Never Seen Before

Cambrian fossil beds contain animals with anatomies straight out of a surreal painting: multiple stalked eyes, funnel-shaped mouths, segmented bodies beyond today's norms. These life forms, from half a billion years ago, show how evolution tried out unimaginable body plans. Think of it as flipping through abandoned sketches of nature's design. Each fossil reveals an ecosystem of forgotten experiments, proving our current fauna is just one of many possible outcomes.

Sleep Experiments Uncovering Nightmares

In sleep labs, electrodes track brain waves as volunteers slumber. Certain patterns align with distressed dreaming, suggesting that analyzing neural activity might decode how nightmares form. A 2020 study found specific brain regions "overheating" during intense nightmares. Understanding these nighttime horrors could lead us to modulate dream content or ease recurring terrors. It's like cracking the code of our private nighttime cinema, unveiling the hidden scripts that shape our inner fears.

Metals That Melt in Your Hand

Picture a metal that liquefies at room temperature, like gallium, melting with your body heat. Such materials hint at flexible electronics and shape-shifting devices. In 2016, a team proposed using gallium-based alloys for "soft" antennas. The concept shatters our notion of rigid metals. With these substances, hardware could adapt and flow, fueling futuristic visions where technology morphs at will, turning something as solid as metal into a versatile, living resource.

A Robot That Learns Like a Child

In cognitive robotics labs, engineers design robots that don't follow rigid programs but learn like infants. They observe, attempt, err, and retry, as if guided by curiosity. In 2019, a prototype recognized objects simply by watching other robots "play." This shrinks the gap between AI and human learning. Instead of cold instructions, robots absorb knowledge through experience, hinting at a future where they grow more like students than machines, and intelligence sprouts naturally, like a young mind exploring a toy box.

Mini-Brains Grown in Test Tubes

Brain organoids, tiny spheres of stem cells grown in vitro, mimic early brain development. In 2018, researchers noted spontaneous neural waves in these miniature "brains." They aren't conscious, but crucial for studying conditions like Alzheimer's without testing on animals or humans. Observing these cellular clusters is like peering into the mind's first sparks. A path to unravel neurological puzzles and approach the essence of thought at its embryonic stage.

Genetic Engineering and 'Spider Goats'

Imagine goats with spider genes producing milk rich in spider-silk-like proteins. No sci-fi: this is real genetic tweaking. The resulting fiber rivals steel in strength and lightness, a material beyond natural limits. This fusion of DNA from distant species is a bold leap, raising ethical and technological questions. It's evolution hacked by human hands, forging new biological hybrids to meet our material desires — an unsettling but astonishing outcome of scientific ingenuity.

Microbes That Feast on Plastic

Plastic, an environmental scourge, might meet its match in certain bacteria that degrade it. Discovered in 2016, these microbes can munch on PET, hinting at a future bio-solution to waste. They're microscopic heroes turning mountains of trash into something manageable. Though not a magic bullet, it's a hopeful sign that biology might help clear the clutter. A minuscule army battling our colossal mess, offering a glimpse of harmony restored.

Artificial Volcanoes in the Lab

To predict real volcanic threats, researchers recreate mini-eruptions with synthetic lava in controlled setups. By filming how flows form and spread, they learn to model actual disasters. It's a serious game: scaling down nature's fury to a desktop experiment helps us anticipate real pyroclastic dangers. Just think: by playing with molten analogs, we decipher the logic of fiery giants, turning destructive chaos into knowledge that might save lives.

Giant Telescopes in Underground Caves

To detect elusive cosmic particles, scientists hide detectors deep underground, where Earth's bulk filters out interference. It's a counterintuitive approach: studying the universe by burrowing down. In 2015, a mine-based detector spotted signals otherwise lost in cosmic noise. Like reversing astronomy's usual gaze, it proves that sometimes you must go inward to comprehend the cosmos. An upside-down stargazing that expands the toolkit of exploration.

Physics Labs on Space Stations

In orbit, materials and fluids behave in unexpected ways. In 2020, an ISS experiment observed crystal patterns impossible under Earth's gravity. Microgravity unveils phenomena masked down here. To truly know nature's laws, sometimes we must leave our planet, drifting in vacuum to see how matter and energy dance without gravity's constant tug. It's a reminder: for deep comprehension, we must dare to step off our world's stage. What we find out there can surprise us, making us realize the universe always holds another trick up its cosmic sleeve.

Chapter 14:
Literature, Authors & Unusual Books

Famous Novelists with Secret Pen Names

Did you know that some very famous authors published novels under assumed names, just to see how readers would react without their star status shining overhead? J.K. Rowling, for instance, wrote detective stories as Robert Galbraith, and the secret only leaked months after the book's modest arrival in stores. In the 19th century, Mary Ann Evans became George Eliot to be taken seriously in a male-dominated literary scene. It's as if these writers wore literary masks to leave their comfort zones, testing their skill without the weight of their own reputations. A playful identity game revealing the complex ego hidden behind the pen.

Encrypted Manuscripts Never Deciphered

The Voynich Manuscript is the most famous example: a 15th-century illustrated codex written in an unknown script and stuffed with impossible plants and cryptic diagrams. Modern cryptographers and AI have failed to decode it. And it's not alone: texts like the Rohonczi Codex remain inscrutable riddles. Some suspect elaborate pranks, others see esoteric lore or lost knowledge. These mysterious works are literary ghosts we cannot interpret, showing that written words can become impenetrable puzzles, a perpetual invitation to find a nonexistent key.

Floating Libraries on Ships

Not all libraries rest on solid ground. Since the 20th century, some ships have been turned into floating book havens, sailing along rivers or coasts to bring reading material to isolated villages or remote islands. Norway's "Epos" library boat delivers literature to distant fjord communities. International projects load thousands of volumes onto vessels, making the ocean a channel for culture. This blend of maritime adventure and printed knowledge proves that reading can reach anyone, anywhere—even where civilization feels far away.

Books Forbidden and Burned Through the Ages

History is littered with texts tossed onto the pyre: censored by regimes, churches, or ideologies that feared their ideas. From the burned Library of Alexandria to the Nazi bonfires of "degenerate" literature, oppression often targets words. The 1564 Index of Forbidden Books tried to save souls by banning titles. Ironically, censorship often grants these works legendary status, boosting curiosity. Every burned book is a scar, but also proof of literature's power: no matter how many flames are lit, the spark of knowledge endures.

Poetry Written on Leaves and Bark

Before paper, some cultures etched verses on palm leaves or tree bark. In ancient India, sacred texts were engraved on plant fibers; in Polynesia, certain barks carried poems. Writing adapted to what nature offered, making literature a biological act. It's as if poetry sprouted from the environment itself, blossoming from branches rather than shelves. A reminder that the written word can thrive anywhere, taking root among trees and whispering from the rustle of leaves.

Authors Who Hated Their Most Famous Works

Odd but true: some writers loathed the books that made them famous. Arthur Conan Doyle grew sick of Sherlock Holmes, a character he deemed too trivial compared to his loftier ambitions. Ian Fleming found some Bond stories shallow and tiresome. These authors, trapped by their own success, resented the label that defined them. It's funny to think that a beloved masterpiece can be a burden to its creator. It reveals the paradox of genius: the celebrated hit might become a cage, leaving the artist irked by their own acclaim.

Novels Generated by Algorithms

With AI's rise, some novels are now written by software. In 2016, a computer-generated story even reached the preliminary rounds of a Japanese literary prize. These experiments challenge our notions: what makes a text "human"? If a machine can produce coherent narratives, is creativity still uniquely ours? Maybe we're seeing a new hybrid literature, where the author is a curator and the computer an assistant, stretching the boundaries between biological mind and digital logic.

Stories Transmitted Only Orally

Long before writing, entire cultures lived on spoken tales. Epics, legends, and sagas were memorized by bards and storytellers, passed down through generations. The Odyssey was likely sung aloud for centuries before being inked. Even today, in certain tribes, oral tradition preserves ancient lore, mental maps of the land, and complex genealogies. It's a literature of voice, without physical supports—an art of listening and spoken memory. Fragile yet alive, it proves words can survive without ink or screens, thriving in memory's embrace.

The World's Strangest Bookstores

Some bookstores reside in old phone booths, filled with donated paperbacks. In Colombia, a traveling library rides on a donkey to mountain hamlets. In Spain, a secret cave harbors rare volumes. It's the creativity of the traveling bookseller, proving readers can be anywhere. These unusual spots show that seeking knowledge needs no fancy halls: a tucked-away nook or a roaming shelf suffices. Passion for words does the rest.

Biographies of Imaginary Animals

Imagine a book detailing the life and deeds of creatures that never existed: dragons with intricate family trees, unicorns with childhood anecdotes. These "biographies" of fictional beasts challenge our notion of non-fiction, blending reality's style with fantasy's core. A literary trick: credibility rests on tone, not truth. This fearless imagination turns the boundary between fact and invention into a playful playground where we can believe, if only momentarily, that nonexistent beings breathe on the page.

Inks Made from Improbable Substances

In the past, ink could come from cuttlefish, oak galls, crushed insects, or even body fluids in extreme cases. Medieval scribes experimented with minerals and plant extracts for unique hues. Fascinating that ancient manuscripts owe their colors to such odd recipes. It's a reminder that writing wasn't always a luxury, but a craft of adaptation and resourcefulness. The pen could be born from marine creatures, the word from a pigment conjured out of nature's cupboard.

Stories Illustrated by Child Prodigies

Not all renowned illustrators are seasoned adults. Some editions feature drawings by extraordinarily young talents. Picture a 10-year-old who paints a classic tale with a naïve, fresh vision. These encounters between mature texts and a child's hand yield peculiar editions: old words gain renewed vitality through innocent colors. Talent has no age, and literature can open its doors to unexpected collaborations, enriching the reading experience with youthful wonder.

Books Without Vowels

Ernest Vincent Wright's "Gadsby" avoided using the letter 'e.' Other writers tried similarly daunting constraints. Such texts reveal language's malleability: strip it of a crucial letter and it still speaks.

The reader may feel challenged, yet intrigued by this intellectual game that tests the borders of expression. Like a linguistic gym, these vowel-shy or letter-free experiments prove that words can shine under the toughest conditions, unveiling fresh nuances.

Interactive Stories with Multiple Endings

Before video games, "choose-your-own-adventure" books let readers pick paths, shaping the narrative's direction. A single novel might offer ten endings, a labyrinth of choices. This playful concept anticipated today's hypertext fiction, where links replace chapters. The reader co-authors the tale by selecting outcomes. A forerunner of narrative gaming, it shows how literature can share storytelling power, making the audience an active participant rather than a passive spectator.

Authors Who Wrote Only at Night

Some writers preferred darkness: Gustave Flaubert loved the quiet after midnight; Jane Austen wrote in the common room, hiding her pages when someone entered. These habits reveal an intimate dimension of creation. The author is no machine but a person with routines, quirks, even superstitions. Knowing a great novel emerged at 1 a.m. by lamplight adds human texture to the work, reminding us that behind every page lies a real heartbeat.

Novels Printed on Recycled Old Newspapers

Limited editions sometimes use eco-friendly supports, like paper recycled from old newspapers. The new story overlaps faded headlines and photos, blending past and present. In 2020, an indie publisher printed a short story on '60s newspaper sheets, creating a collage of eras. It's a symbolic fusion: the book as an artifact that embraces history, reusing what once conveyed daily facts to carry fresh fiction. A sustainable and poetic way to give words another life.

Anthologies of Nonsense Phrases

There are collections of aphorisms without any logical sense, phrases that mean nothing yet evoke bizarre images, like "The sun bounces on the hat of the wind." These surreal stylistic exercises celebrate absurdity, challenging our standard idea of communication. Freed from meaning, language becomes pure sound and image. Readers, disoriented, rediscover that not every sentence must be rational; sometimes, writing can be a playground of whimsical nonsense, a feast for imagination.

Love Letters Between Rival Authors

Imagine two famous writers, publicly at odds, exchanging private, tender letters. Such cases exist: intellectual adversaries who, behind the scenes, confessed respect and affection. Like duelists who, in front of the crowd, cross swords, but in private share admiration. It's a paradox revealing human complexity: beyond literary feuds lie intricate personal bonds. Rivalries and debates can coexist with warmth, reminding us that people, not just ideas, shape the literary landscape.

Unique Copies of Books Lost Forever

Some manuscripts were one-of-a-kind and vanished in fires, wars, or neglect. Mentioned in ancient catalogs, they survive only as rumors. These "bibliographic ghosts" fascinate us: the idea that a masterpiece vanished without leaving a copy. In a world of digital duplications, imagining a unique text consumed by flames highlights how each book can be an irreplaceable treasure. A wistful reminder that knowledge can slip through our fingers, irretrievable.

The Shortest Novel and the Longest Story

"For sale: baby shoes, never worn" is often cited as a super-short story, possibly by Hemingway, packing immense emotion into just six words. On the other side, sprawling sagas span thousands of pages, engaging readers for months. This contrast shows that length doesn't define narrative impact. A tiny phrase can strike deeper than a multi-volume epic. Literature defies measurement: a handful of syllables can hold a universe.

Chapter 15:
Wonders of the Body & Curious Wellness Tips

Medicinal Plants Grown on Rooftops

In certain rural or mountainous villages, rooftops aren't just for sheltering from rain—they can serve as tiny suspended gardens. Up there, among tiles and shingles, locals grow medicinal herbs like thyme, oregano, wild mint, or chamomile. This tradition isn't just about using every inch of space, it represents a synergy between architecture and nature: the roof becomes a healing garden. So, when a family needs a calming decoction or a digestive infusion, they just climb up a ladder, pick a few fresh leaves, and brew a tea. A small ecosystem at one's fingertips, blending rural life and ancient remedies.

Massages Performed with Ice Stones

Not only hot stones have a place in luxury spas. In some Northern European or northern Asian cultures, therapists use ice-cold stones to massage the body. The idea is controlled thermal shock: skin exposed to intense cold reacts by stimulating circulation and "waking up" from sluggish blood flow. Some athletes use it to recover after intense exertion—an extreme twist on the classic ice pack. The result is a feeling of vigor and lightness, as if the body finds a new equilibrium between shiver and relaxation.

Intermittent Fasting in Ancient Times

Modern trendy intermittent fasting has deep historical roots. Ancient civilizations practiced fasting for centuries to purify both body and mind. Egyptians dedicated certain days to bodily cleansing, Greeks believed fasting could sharpen intellect, and Buddhist monks limited their meals to specific hours. It wasn't about dieting, but harmony: taming instincts, elevating the spirit. Some tribes treated it as a rite of passage testing personal will. Surprising how a "new trend" actually echoes age-old traditions, bridging today's wellness hype and venerable cultural practices.

Grandma's Remedies for Toothache

Before dentists and modern anesthetics, how did people ease toothache? Grandmothers recommended chewing cloves for their natural numbing effect, or applying bitter roots to the gum. Some cultures used vinegar-salt rinses or sage leaves. Others pressed crushed garlic near the sore tooth. Primitive and not always effective, these methods show human ingenuity in facing pain with whatever was at hand. Today they may make us smile, but back then they were the only immediate relief—and a testament to human resilience and inventiveness.

Desert Saunas

In certain desert regions, the idea of a sauna takes an unexpected form. No wood or steam, just a hole dug in scorching sand. You lie inside, partially covered, letting the sun's heat make you sweat. It's a natural sauna under open skies. No eucalyptus aroma, but the intense heat and abundant sweat give a sense of purification. This ancestral method turns an extreme environment into a free wellness spot. Where water is scarce, the desert itself becomes a spa, merging harsh nature and bodily detox.

Yoga Suspended in Midair

Yoga isn't confined to a mat on the floor. "Aerial yoga" uses hammocks hung from the ceiling, making inverted or complex poses easier thanks to reduced gravity. The feeling is of floating, as if the body forgets its weight. This practice fuses yoga, aerial dance, and fitness, mixing relaxation and fun. Practitioners say the "upside-down" perspective refreshes the mind. An antigravity experience that turns the studio into a cozy nest, gently rewriting the rules of gravity.

Thermal Treatments with Volcanic Mud

Thermal springs in volcanic areas yield mud rich in minerals: sulfur, iron, silica. Applying it to the skin is an ancient ritual. In Iceland or Japan, people cover themselves with this mineral-packed sludge to improve circulation, soothe joint pain, and soften the skin. It's like a caress from the Earth's core, bathing in primordial nature. Standing in a warm, sulfur-scented mud bath connects you to the planet's depths, blending geology with well-being in a timeless ritual of natural therapy.

Massages with Snakes,

In some spas, instead of hot stones or expert hands, non-venomous snakes glide over the client's back. An extreme experience, playing on the tactile sensation of cool, slithering skin and the emotional challenge of facing a primal fear. Those who've tried it report an initial adrenaline rush followed by relief. It's not for everyone, but it shows how humans push boundaries: transforming ancient terror into a paradoxical relaxation tool. A meeting point of courage, curiosity, and nature in the form of a massage.

Acupuncture with Fish Spines?

Before metal needles, some traditions used sharp natural objects like fish spines to stimulate body points. A rudimentary preview of sophisticated Chinese acupuncture. The idea that a simple animal spine could balance internal flows proves human adaptability. Today's acupuncture is refined, but recalling these primitive ancestors pays homage to the creativity behind these techniques— born perhaps from trial and error closer to nature than medical labs.

Breathing Techniques Against Stress

Long before wellness apps, ancient methods calmed body and mind through mere breath control. Pranayama in yoga, Zen deep breathing, or the "4-7-8" technique to counter anxiety—all show that slowing the breath lowers heart rate and stress hormones. It's an ancient weapon against tension, needing no tools or expense. A vital act elevated to a balancing art. Life begins and ends with a breath; between those two extremes, we can find serenity by simply managing the air we inhale and exhale.

Therapeutic Forests

In Japan they call it "shinrin-yoku," forest bathing. No swimming involved—just sensorial immersion: walking slowly among trees, listening to rustling leaves, smelling moss, watching dappled light. Studies show reduced stress and boosted immunity. It's like plugging into green energy, escaping hyper-technology for pure greenery. The forest's silent conversation restores us, an invisible medicine whispered by branches and roots, reminding us that to heal we might step out of concrete boxes into living woods.

Unusual Hiccup Cures

Who hasn't tried a bizarre trick to stop hiccups? Drinking water upside down, startling the sufferer, holding your breath, or sucking on a spoonful of sugar—each culture has odd methods. Not always effective, but hiccups are so trivial and annoying that we'll try anything. In the past, gently pulling the tongue or massaging the nape were suggested. Perhaps no perfect remedy exists, but these whimsical attempts turn the search for relief into a test of creativity and laughter.

Cleopatra's Donkey Milk Baths in Antiquity

Cleopatra reportedly bathed in donkey's milk, believing it to soften and rejuvenate her skin. Rich in vitamins and fatty acids, donkey milk was then a luxury reserved for queens and aristocrats. Today it sounds extravagant, but once it was the "deluxe cosmetics" of the past. Legend or truth, it fuses history, beauty, and exotic flair. A ritual that shows how past societies sourced body care from unexpected ingredients, blending myth and skincare before modern lotions existed.

Swing-Based Workouts for Balance

A swing isn't just child's play. Some modern trainers use swings for balance and strength exercises: standing on the seat, doing squats or lunges while it sways. In 2018, a study found 10 minutes on a swing could improve proprioception. Turning a childhood pastime into a fitness tool adds fun and challenge. It's a nostalgic return to innocence, discovering new ways to build muscle and coordination through gentle back-and-forth motion.

Little-Known Anti-Stress Foods

Not just chamomile or valerian. Certain cultures treasure rare roots, wild mushrooms, or mountain berries considered "adaptogens," helping the body cope with stress. Ashwagandha in India or reishi mushrooms in the East have long reputations. Though not always scientifically confirmed, their fame endures for centuries. The appeal lies in seeking natural serenity without drugs, finding culinary secrets passed down verbally. Each nibble of these mysterious foods may carry ancient wisdom hidden in every bite.

Curing Insomnia with Whale Sounds

Falling asleep lulled by deep whale calls? Some apps and alternative therapies propose natural soundscapes—rain, nocturnal forests, whale songs—to combat insomnia. By recreating soothing auditory contexts, they try to counter urban noise. Whale melodies, with their profound rhythms, evoke an oceanic vastness that envelops and calms. No definitive scientific proof, but many swear it works. It's poetic: letting marine world lull us to peaceful slumber, replacing city chaos with aquatic lullabies.

Scalp Massages with Bone Combs

In ancient times, head massages used tools carved from bone or wood. Gentle strokes over the scalp improved circulation and relieved tension. Imagine skilled hands guiding a handcrafted comb, transforming daily grooming into relaxation. Today it's niche, but the idea of enhancing a simple routine like brushing your hair into a wellness ritual is captivating. Ancestral wisdom suggests not to underestimate small gestures that can deliver moments of pure ease and contentment.

Ritual Fasting and Effects on the Mind

Fasting in many religions isn't just physical—it's spiritual. Hindu ascetics, Christian monks, Sufi mystics—they all refrain from food for reasons beyond health: to purify the soul, fortify willpower, enter altered mental states. Fasting becomes a bridge between body and mind, a disciplined sacrifice releasing hidden strength. It's not about losing weight but finding inner clarity, a link to ancient times where withholding nourishment was a tool for growth and deeper insight.

Aromatic Essences as Natural 'Vaccines'

Before modern immunizations, some communities tried to "inoculate" against illnesses by burning aromatic plants and resins, believing their pungent fumes protective. Though not scientific by today's standards, it was an ingenious attempt to harness nature's antimicrobial hints. Historians suggest these rituals might have at least reduced humidity or repelled insect vectors. A fragrant ancestor of today's vaccines, showing how humans have always sought preventive measures, even if guided more by scent and ritual than lab tests.

Eye Exercises for Hawk-Like Vision

Before glasses and screens, people trained their eyes by shifting focus between near and far objects or tracking moving targets. Ancient archers honed their eyesight to detect distant prey. Such techniques resurface today to relieve digital eye strain. Gently rotating the gaze, following something in motion, or staring at green fields can relax eye muscles. A soothing balm for weary eyes, a return to a nearly forgotten gymnastics for vision, reminding us that even our gaze can be trained, flexible, and refreshed.

Chapter 16:
Debunking Myths & Urban Legends

A Glass of Water on the TV

In some homes, especially in certain rural areas or among superstitious folks, you might spot a glass of water placed on top of the TV or a high shelf. The belief is that this water "absorbs" negative energies or purifies the atmosphere, acting like a simple talisman. There's no scientific basis: water doesn't possess mystical powers in this context, nor does the TV emit strange forces. It's pure superstition—perhaps a comforting gesture that provides psychological relief. Habits like these survive to reassure people, not because they produce real effects. If you see a glass perched up there, know that it's just symbolic reassurance, not a magic purifier.

Does Chewing Gum Stay in Your Stomach for Years?

A common myth claims that swallowing gum leaves it stuck in your stomach for seven years. In reality, while gum can't be digested, it passes through the intestines and is eventually expelled, usually within a few days. No gluey lumps remain for years. This belief likely arose to scare kids into not swallowing gum. The truth is simpler: gum is inert and just moves along like other indigestible items. No blockages, no long-term residue, just a false alarm.

Is the Sea Really Trapped in a Seashell's Sound?

When you hold a seashell to your ear and hear a distant roar, many believe it's the captured sound of the ocean. Actually, what you hear is a mix of ambient noise and the sound of your own blood flow, amplified by the shell's shape. The shell acts as a resonator for surrounding sounds. There's no ocean inside, just an acoustic illusion. As children, we're enchanted; as adults, we learn the truth. The shell is a tiny echo chamber, not a conch of the deep sea.

Frogs Raining from the Sky

Stories of frogs, fish, or small animals falling from the sky sound like tall tales, but there's a scientific explanation. Occasionally, tornadoes or waterspouts can suck animals from ponds or streams and deposit them far away. When the whirlwind's energy wanes, the creatures "rain" down, creating the illusion of animal rainfall. Not a miracle, just a rare meteorological event. So if you hear about frogs dropping from the sky, think of a mischievous tornado, not a supernatural downpour.

Is the Toilet Seat the Dirtiest Place?

People often assume the toilet seat is the filthiest spot in the house, but tests have shown that objects like keyboards, phones, and kitchen sponges can host more bacteria. While hygiene is key, it's misguided to panic about the toilet seat alone. Regular cleaning and handwashing suffice. Don't fixate only on the "poor" toilet—many everyday items can be even dirtier. The real secret? Good hygiene habits, without singling out one "culprit."

Do Goldfish Really Have a Memory of Mere Seconds?

The myth that goldfish remember only a few seconds has been debunked by studies. These little swimmers can learn routines, recognize feeding signals, and retain information for days or weeks. Experiments with timed feeding showed they "waited" at the right hour. They're not geniuses, but not amnesiac fools either. This stereotype probably arises from their simple appearance. Science reveals a more complex creature than popular lore suggests.

Does Sugar Make Children Hyperactive?

At birthday parties, kids get wild after sweets, and we blame the sugar. But scientific studies find no direct link between sugar intake and hyperactivity. The excitement likely comes from the party atmosphere, the thrill of celebration, not the sugar itself. Of course, too many sweets aren't healthy, but to pin all that energy on sugar alone is a convenient myth. Context and emotion count more than a spoonful of sugar.

Does Cutting Your Hair Make It Grow Back Stronger?

Many believe that trimming hair makes it grow thicker and stronger. In reality, cutting doesn't affect the hair shaft's structure or the root in the scalp. Hair seems sturdier only because the shorter part is less worn. There's no magical hair-strengthening scissor effect. Hair quality depends on genetics, nutrition, and health, not on how often you visit the barber. It's an optical illusion: shorter hair appears more robust, but that's it.

Do Lightning Bolts Never Strike the Same Place Twice?

The saying "Lightning never strikes twice" is a myth. Lightning rods, tall towers, and skyscrapers are hit repeatedly. Lightning follows the path of least electrical resistance; if a spot favors that path, it can be struck multiple times. Tall buildings often get hit many times over the years. Nature doesn't care about proverbs. This folk saying has no basis in physics—lightning can and does return to the same spot.

Do Ostriches Bury Their Heads in the Sand?

The image of an ostrich hiding its head underground to avoid danger is pure myth. Ostriches lower their heads to check on eggs or peck at the ground, not to "ignore" threats. The romantic idea of a cowardly ostrich is a misunderstanding. In reality, ostriches have other defense strategies, like running fast or kicking. No head-burying is needed— just another legend turned into common "knowledge."

Do Hair Turn White Suddenly After a Shock?

No documented case shows hair turning white overnight from fright. Graying is a gradual process tied to genetics, age, and hormonal factors. Stories of sudden whitening are legends. Shock or fear doesn't instantly strip pigment. The body doesn't operate like a paintbrush. Perhaps confusion arises from cases where lighter roots become visible after a haircut, but it's not a magical bleaching caused by terror.

Were the Pyramids Built by Aliens?

Sensational theories claim aliens built the Egyptian pyramids, assuming ancient humans weren't capable. Archeology, however, extensively documents the methods, tools, and organizational skills of ancient Egyptians. No extraterrestrial intervention required. Ingenious techniques, labor, and mathematics suffice to explain these monuments. Believing in aliens stems from underestimating our ancestors, not from any real evidence.

Is Eating Before Swimming Dangerous?

The myth that eating before swimming leads to fatal cramps lacks strong evidence. Sure, a heavy meal before diving into cold water may feel uncomfortable, but there's no scientific ban on a light swim after a snack. The fear likely arose as a cautionary tale. Just listen to your body—if you feel good, a gentle swim after a sandwich isn't deadly. A sensible approach, not an absolute rule.

Miracle Mud Packs to Instantly Lose Fat?

Believing that a mud wrap can dissolve fat instantly is wishful thinking. At best, you lose temporary water weight, making skin appear firmer. The fat doesn't melt away. This marketing myth sells quick fixes that don't exist. Real weight loss requires a calorie deficit and exercise, not magical mud. Mud treatments can relax or improve circulation superficially, but no radical fat burning. It's a spa fantasy, not a scientific method.

Do Vaccines Cause Absurd Diseases?

Conspiracy theories claim vaccines trigger bizarre illnesses. Science repeatedly disproves such nonsense: vaccines are among the safest and most effective health tools. No autism, no microchips, no strange pathologies. Billions of data points confirm their safety. These rumors thrive on misinformation and fear of the unknown. Trust reputable sources to dispel these tales and protect ourselves and our communities.

Is There a Safe Time to Stare at the Sun?

No time of day makes looking directly at the sun safe. Even a glance can damage the retina irreversibly. Some think certain hours are harmless—wrong. Solar radiation always harms. Experts insist on adequate eye protection or filters. Don't risk your sight. The sun's brightness is constant danger to unshielded eyes, no matter the hour.

Hairdryer in the Bathtub: Just a Myth?

There's no myth here: dropping a hairdryer in the bath or touching electrical devices with wet hands is truly dangerous. Water and electricity don't mix. This isn't an urban legend—it's real risk. Safety rules exist for a reason. Electric shock in water scenarios is deadly, not a rumor. Follow common sense and stay safe.

Sleeping with Plants in the Room is Dangerous?

Some worry that having plants in the bedroom at night steals too much oxygen. In reality, their O_2 consumption at night is minimal and not harmful. A couple of plants won't threaten your health. The idea that they "rob" air is unfounded. Plants can even improve humidity and daytime air quality. Another fear dismissed by actual evidence.

Spinach as an Extraordinary Source of Iron

The myth that spinach is iron-rich originated from a misplaced decimal in an old study, inflating its iron content. Popeye and pop culture cemented this belief, but spinach isn't the iron powerhouse we imagined. Though still nutritious, it's not a miracle food of iron. A tiny mistake became a giant nutritional legend.

The Great Wall Visible from Space?

People say the Great Wall of China is the only human structure visible to the naked eye from space. Astronauts have refuted this claim. Without tools, distinguishing man-made details from orbit is tough, and the Great Wall is no exception. This myth likely began to praise the monument's grandeur. In reality, Earth's large-scale features, not individual constructions, are what stand out.

Chapter 17:
Outdoor Oddities & Survival Secrets

Plants That Thrive in the Impossible

In certain corners of the world, plants survive under conditions that would baffle any engineer: cacti enduring years without rain, ferns clinging to the bare cliffs of the Andes, or mosses thriving in soils laden with heavy metals. Near Chernobyl, some plants have adapted their DNA to withstand radiation, turning a nuclear nightmare into a peculiar evolutionary trial. A study found that about 75% of these extreme species display unusual genetic mutations. It's as if nature toys with its own limits, proving that even amid radiation, drought, and toxins, the plant kingdom always finds a foothold for life.

Finding Your Way Without Compass or GPS

Before the digital era, explorers navigated by subtle hints in the landscape. Moss often grows on the damper, shaded side of trees (commonly north), the sun sets in the west, and the North Star points north at night. In Lapland, Sami nomads learned to interpret a stick's shadow to gauge time and direction, while certain oceanic tribes read wave patterns to find remote islands. An anthropologist noted that some ancient cultures could cross thousands of kilometers of desert or open sea without getting lost. It's a reminder that the natural world is a living map, if we know how to read it.

How Animals Survive in Harsh Conditions

The pygmy mouse lemur of Madagascar slows its metabolism nearly to a standstill to endure dry seasons. In the Namib Desert, a beetle harvests morning fog droplets on its armored back for a daily drink. High in the Himalayas, yaks have more efficient hemoglobin to handle thin air. A study on Arctic animals found that 80% adopt strategies like hibernation or ultra-insulation. Each ecosystem is a test, and every creature answers with a special trick. Nature is an endless manual of extreme solutions, showing that every environment is a puzzle life knows how to solve.

Crazy Climates and Incredible Survival Stories

There are tales of people surviving weeks in polar storms, forced to build igloo-like shelters and eat seal blubber. In 1823, a British sailor stranded on a tropical isle survived a full month on coconuts alone. A researcher counted over 200 documented cases of castaways and explorers enduring isolation by improvising: collecting rainwater in wooden crates, using mud as insect repellent, snacking on crunchy insects for protein. These accounts prove human ingenuity can outsmart even the most hostile climates. Each event becomes a lesson in how far determination and cleverness can carry us in nature's harshest arenas.

Edible Wild Foods You Never Considered

In jungles or steppes, nature's pantry is filled with foods we often overlook. Certain beetle larvae pack more protein than a boiled egg. Some Amazonian tribes savor giant ants for their amino acids. In Central Asian grasslands, nomads know which wild roots can feed entire families during droughts. Ethnobotanical surveys show that up to 80% of "non-food" species to modern humans were vital staples for our ancestors. It's like a hidden supermarket: with the right know-how, you can distinguish nourishing morsels from deadly ones. In emergencies, this ancient knowledge can turn the wilderness into a buffet of unexpected sustenance.

Filtering Water with Your T-Shirt

In an emergency, lacking high-tech filters, a simple piece of cotton can help. Pouring murky water through your shirt removes sand, bugs, and larger debris. Then, boiling the filtered water kills most bacteria. A survey of explorers and soldiers shows about 60% know this basic trick. It's not perfect, but a start toward potable water. A rudimentary solution that, in a pinch, proves effective if nothing else is available. Survival often hinges on simple ideas born of necessity, reminding us that human resourcefulness can turn a scrap of fabric into a lifesaver.

Communicating at a Distance with Smoke Signals

Before radios and smartphones, smoke signals served as a form of visual telecommunication. Apache tribes used them to warn of strangers; ancient Chinese watchtowers did the same for enemy troops. An ethnologist found at least 40 different cultures employing smoke and fabric to modulate messages. It was enough to say "Danger" or "I need help" across valleys and hillsides. Though it can't convey poetry, in extreme situations it might still help. It's a return to ancestral simplicity, where a puff of smoke is an exclamation mark in the sky—communication stripped to its elemental essence.

Frogs Frozen and Revived

In parts of North America, some frogs endure winter by literally freezing their internal fluids. Their hearts stop beating, their blood turns to ice, yet special sugars and proteins prevent cell damage. Come spring, they thaw and hop away as if nothing happened. A biologist found that over 90% survive sub-zero conditions this way. This trick, intriguing researchers studying organ preservation, feels like a biological spell. Nature, yet again, bends the rules of life and death, turning freezing into a perfect survival strategy and inspiring humans to rethink what's possible in preserving life.

Tree Resin as Natural Glue

Long before synthetic adhesives, people relied on tree resin. Slightly heated, it forms a sticky paste to fix tools, seal containers, or bind arrowheads to shafts. Archaeologists discovered prehistoric arrowheads with resin traces dating back 20,000 years. In emergencies, a dab of resin can mend a broken utensil, making the difference between going hungry and having dinner. Resin was the "super glue" of ancient times, a natural adhesive provided by the forest. It shows that before chemical labs, humans had their resourceful workshop in the woods.

Fishing with Rudimentary Traps

Without modern rods or hooks, our ancestors still caught fish. Stacking stones to create a low dam in a stream, they funneled fish into small pools. Making funnel-shaped traps from flexible branches or using mildly toxic leaves to stun fish were also methods employed by various tribes. An ethnologist noted that at least 50 indigenous groups on different continents used such techniques. It's the art of exploiting water flow and simple structures to secure a meal. No fancy gear needed, just a keen understanding of rivers and currents.

Cooking Over Fire Without Pots

No metal pot? No problem. You can heat stones in a fire to serve as a makeshift grill. Wrap food in green leaves for a natural steamer, or use sharp sticks as skewers. Native Americans and Australian Aboriginals cooked fish on hot rocks or meat in earthen pits lined with leaves. Anthropologists estimate that about 70% of pre-metal societies had ingenious cooking methods. This reminds us that cuisine isn't born in a kitchen—it's forged in the wild, with stone, wood, and leaf serving as utensils.

Nutrient-Rich Insects in the Forest

Ants, grasshoppers, and larvae offer protein, B vitamins, and minerals. The FAO estimates that over 2 billion people already eat insects, seeing them as a valuable, affordable protein source. To our modern Western eyes it may seem odd, but in survival scenarios, knowing which bugs to eat can be a lifesaver. Termites, for instance, boast protein levels rivaling beef. This perspective shift turns a forest floor into a pantry. In a pinch, that wriggly larva might mean the difference between hunger and strength.

Testing a Berry for Poison

In dire circumstances, if you must test an unknown berry, tradition suggests observing animals first, then rubbing a tiny piece on your skin, and finally tasting a minuscule amount and waiting hours for a reaction. It's risky and not recommended unless desperate. Indigenous peoples relied on cumulative wisdom; today it's a last resort. Approximately 30% of wild plants can be toxic. Without proper knowledge, it's a gamble. The moral: better learn safe plant identification in advance rather than play botanical roulette.

Interpreting Animal Tracks

Footprints, droppings, scratch marks on trees—reading these signs is like flipping through a silent field guide. A deer's track might mean water nearby, wolf prints hint at predators and prey interactions, scattered feathers tell of a raptor's meal. Some hunter-gatherer societies, like those in the Kalahari, identify over 200 types of tracks. Without GPS, these clues become your living atlas. Tracks reveal who shares your environment, helping you find resources or avoid danger. Nature's cryptic messages, waiting for those who know how to listen with their eyes.

Recognizing Local Medicinal Plants

Indigenous communities used leaves, roots, and barks as their pharmacy. The Amazon's bark to reduce fever, Alpine flowers to soothe bruises—each region has its green remedies. Ethnobotanists have cataloged thousands of healing species known to native peoples. Without modern drugs, a simple leaf could ease pain or disinfect a wound. This knowledge, partly overshadowed by modern medicine, is now intriguing researchers. In emergencies, knowing which plant to chew might save you from suffering. A treasure of ancient wisdom, bridging humanity's past and present in every forest clearing.

Making Rope from Plant Fibers

Without synthetic rope, tying a shelter or hoisting a load would be tough. Yet nature offers fibers: stinging nettle, wild hemp, or flax. Twisting and braiding them creates surprisingly strong cords. Archeologists found traces of plant-based cords in prehistoric sites, proving technology began with the right plant, not metal tools. In survival, crafting a rope from leaves and bark is like summoning an invisible helper. It's about transforming raw nature into a useful tool, using patient hands to weave your lifeline from the green tapestry around you.

Preserving Food Without a Fridge

Smoking fish over aromatic wood, drying mushrooms in the sun, salting meat to draw out moisture: ancient methods allowed long-term storage. Vikings used ice and snow, Bedouins dried dates for desert treks. An anthropologist found that at least 70% of traditional cultures had inventive preservation methods. These approaches defy the idea that without electricity we starve. Just a bit of smoke, salt, or a cool cave suffices to stretch food supplies through harsh seasons. A culinary wisdom older than any freezer, ensuring survival in times of scarcity.

Purifying Water by Boiling Stones

If you have no metal pot, you can still boil water. Heating stones in a fire, then dropping them into a hollowed piece of wood or animal hide container raises the water's temperature enough to kill germs. Prehistoric peoples used this trick, as documented by artifact residues. It's almost magical: no metal needed, just fire and rock, turning contaminated water into something safe. Another lesson from history: simplicity can achieve sterility, and ancient ingenuity offers solutions that modern minds might find surprisingly elegant.

Predicting Weather by Watching Clouds

Observing cumulus or cirrus clouds can forecast rain or shine. Farmers and shepherds passed down these skills for centuries. Wispy cirrus often signal an approaching front, low grey clouds hint at imminent showers. A Swiss meteorologist discovered that Alpine communities predicted the weather with about 70% accuracy just by reading the sky. No apps, just eyes turned upward. Clouds become an ancient weather report, letting you plan your outdoor day. Relearning this old "language" can reconnect us with a world where nature's signals are as reliable as any digital forecast.

Facing a Bear Encounter

Stumbling upon a wild bear demands caution. Experts suggest not running (the bear is faster), not looking it straight in the eye, and not flailing wildly. Speak calmly, back away slowly, appear larger by opening your jacket. A biologist who studied Alaskan predator behavior noted that 80% of encounters end peacefully if you remain composed. The bear may be curious, not aggressive. There's no guarantee, but it's advice born of observation. It's a moment of tension where human reason meets raw nature. Sometimes, a respectful posture is all it takes to avoid turning a meeting into a tragedy.

Chapter 18:
Curiosities about Riddles, Puzzles & Brain-Teasers

The Riddle of the Sphinx

The ancient puzzle posed by the Sphinx to Oedipus—"What creature walks on four legs in the morning, two at midday, and three in the evening?"—is just one example of a millennia-old tradition of mental challenges. Already in Mesopotamia, over 4,000 years ago, riddles tested people's wisdom. The Oedipus tale, solved with the answer "man," shows how our mind has long loved grappling with logical conundrums. In the Middle Ages, some noble courts kept secret riddles on parchments to entertain guests. This proves we never stopped enjoying wordplay and mental tests, from ancient myths to modern quiz shows.

Kakuro, Sudoku's Lesser-Known Cousin

Sudoku conquered the world, but Kakuro—less famous—is equally intriguing. It combines the pleasure of crosswords with arithmetic logic: you must fill the grid with numbers that sum up to given targets. Studies show that numeric puzzles like Kakuro sharpen math skills and reduce stress. In Japan, it's almost as popular as Sudoku. A Japanese publisher notes that 30% of Sudoku solvers try Kakuro for a tougher challenge. Though lesser-known, it's perfect for number-lovers who crave a creative mental workout.

Simple Ciphers for Beginners

From Caesar's shift cipher, where each letter moves through the alphabet, to basic substitution codes, secret messages have fascinated kings, spies, and curious kids for centuries. In Roman times, Julius Caesar used his own cipher for secret communications. Today, solving a simple cipher is a fun logic exercise. A U.S. school study found that 85% of students who try a basic cipher enjoy code-breaking. It's like stepping into the mind of someone hiding a secret—a patient, intuitive puzzle that appeals to all ages.

Medieval Riddles on Parchment

In Europe's royal courts of the 13th and 14th centuries, presenting a riddle to guests was refined entertainment. Without the internet, recorded music, or TV, intellectual challenges served as aristocratic quiz shows. Some manuscripts contain collections of poetic riddles used to impress visitors. Solving them required metaphorical thinking. They were oral cultural gems wrapped in a few lines of verse, a way to showcase wit under torchlight in castles, proving that intellectual play predated modern media.

Tangram Puzzles and Impossible Figures

With just seven geometric pieces, the tangram can generate thousands of shapes. A researcher estimated over 6,500 documented configurations. In ancient China, tangrams trained young nobles' spatial thinking. Modern designers draw inspiration from them for innovative architecture. Like M.C. Escher's impossible figures—stairs rising and falling endlessly—tangrams challenge perception. They invite us to look beyond appearances, revealing the mind's flexibility in seeing infinite possibilities in just a handful of shapes.

Ancient Mazes Recreated in Gardens

Renaissance gardens often featured hedge mazes—three-dimensional puzzles. Hampton Court's famous maze, from around 1690, still confuses half its visitors at least once before they escape. Mazes symbolized life's winding path. A landscape architect suggests navigating a maze stimulates brain regions for spatial memory. A green, living puzzle blending exercise and mental agility, reminding us that the fun of riddles can be tactile and immersive, not confined to paper or screens.

Magic Squares and Lucky Numbers

Magic squares, where each row, column, and diagonal sums to the same number, captivate mathematicians and mystics. The ancient Chinese "Lo Shu" square, thousands of years old, is said to bring harmony. In the Renaissance, Albrecht Dürer embedded one in his artwork as a hidden symbol. An Oxford study notes these patterns sharpen numerical reasoning. Some see them as windows to universal harmony. A simple math puzzle transformed into a cosmic metaphor, where each number fits into a perfect order.

Rebus Puzzles Merging Images and Words

Rebus puzzles blend drawings and letters to form phrases or names. In 19th-century popular magazines, they were all the rage; entire families solved them by candlelight. A linguist notes that 60% of those who try a rebus experience a pleasant "aha!" moment. It's a puzzle bridging the visual and verbal worlds. To solve it, you must think unconventionally—breaking language into signs and sounds, then recombining them for a surprising solution that rewards creative insight.

Mental Mind Games

The prisoner's dilemma, a famous game theory paradox, reveals how logic can clash with self-interest and cooperation. Without trust, rational choices lead to worse outcomes. Economists say about 40% of students encountering it for the first time become fascinated. It's a social puzzle that makes us ponder human nature—how reason and greed intersect, and how even rational decisions can fail to achieve the best results. A mirror held up to our moral and strategic instincts.

Gordian Knots

The Gordian knot myth teaches that sometimes an intractable problem can be solved not by patient unraveling but by a bold, unconventional stroke—like Alexander the Great's sword cut. Modern problem-solving often refers to "cutting the Gordian knot" as taking a radical approach. A legacy from ancient lore that still inspires managers, inventors, and strategists to consider that solutions may lie outside traditional logic.

The Barber Paradox

Bertrand Russell's barber paradox (a barber who shaves only those who don't shave themselves) ends in a logical contradiction. No matter how you reason, you hit a dead end. These paradoxes show that pure logic can create infinite loops of confusion. One mathematician called it a snake biting its tail—a reminder that our intellect can concoct problems that logic itself cannot resolve. They serve no practical purpose except to humble our certainty and amuse the curious.

Rubik's Cubes with Impossible Shapes

The classic Rubik's Cube already boasts millions of permutations, but variants with star shapes or extra layers push complexity beyond measure. A collector reports puzzles with 12 faces and astronomical combination counts. Enthusiasts chase world records: a standard cube can be solved in seconds, yet bizarre variants take ages. This endless hunger for new challenges proves the human mind never settles, always seeking the next level of difficulty, shaping abstract cubes that seem forged in parallel dimensions.

Rhymed Riddles in Popular Tradition

In many cultures, riddles are passed down orally, often in poetic form. Shepherds, farmers, and grandmothers share them with children, forging mental connections between generations. A folklore researcher found that in some parts of Africa, evening gatherings revolve around riddles, strengthening community bonds. Solving a rhymed enigma is a dance between mind and language, a ritual that unites young and old, keeping an ancient form of collective entertainment alive.

Interlocking Rings

Metal puzzles with interlinked rings demand both mental logic and manual dexterity. Medieval craftsmen spent hours on these iron mysteries. Today, artisans create intricate metal puzzles like works of art. A Japanese master forged one with 12 tangled rings, solved by only 5 in 1,000 attempts. It's not just brainwork: fingertips learn to feel subtle angles. A bridge between intellect and touch, proving that mental challenges need not be purely cerebral—hands can guide the mind.

3D Chess Variants

Chess is already complex, but adding vertical levels creates 3D variants. Elite players tackling these versions must think in multiple layers, expanding their strategic horizon. A survey of enthusiasts found only 10% of good chess players handle 3D well. It's a challenge that stretches the mind beyond a flat board. An old game evolving into new adventures, showing that even classic puzzles can find ways to reinvent themselves and keep minds sharp.

The Coin-Weighing Puzzle

Finding a lighter counterfeit coin among many with minimal weighings is a classic puzzle in logic. Mathematicians have devised intricate solutions to minimize error. This problem showcases pure deductive reasoning, and solving it brings pride in outsmarting uncertainty. Such puzzles, trivial in appearance, fueled entire branches of math and logic. They remind us how intellectual pleasures can arise from everyday objects turned into conundrums.

Matchstick Puzzles and Everyday Ingenuity

Moving matchsticks to form correct figures or equations dates back to the 19th century. A British publisher released a collection in 1860, and such puzzles still appear in magazines. Simple yet ingenious, they prove you can craft mental challenges from common items. A modern puzzle designer claims about half of all solvers crack these puzzles within 10 minutes, while others struggle for hours. Common matches become keys to unexpected logical doors, showing how creativity hides in the most mundane corners.

Venn Diagrams and Improbable Deductions

Venn diagrams help solve complex logic problems by visually representing sets and their intersections. For instance, "In a village, those wearing white hats eat only rice, black hats only bread..." Drawing overlapping circles clarifies relationships. A university study found a 30% improvement in solving difficult riddles using visuals. It's proof that a good graphic representation can untangle complexity. Riddles aren't just numbers and words, but also shapes and patterns to decode.

The Königsberg Bridges Enigma

In the 18th century, the city of Königsberg had a puzzle: could one cross all seven bridges without repeating any? Euler's solution created graph theory, birthing a new mathematical field. A mundane civic curiosity sparked an entire branch of science, influencing computers, transport, and social networks. A local quirk, turned puzzle, turned into a keystone of math. It shows how ordinary problems can spark extraordinary insights.

Discoveries About Paper Puzzles and Ingenious Origami

Origami and flexagons transform a simple sheet of paper into objects that morph shape, revealing new sides when folded just right. A flexagon can show more faces than seems geometrically possible. A Princeton mathematician in the 1950s unraveled their secrets. Amazing how a humble sheet can become a multidimensional riddle, a theater of dynamic geometry. It's an example of how human ingenuity sees the extraordinary in the everyday—transforming a square of paper into a challenge for our imaginations.

Chapter 19:
Time, the Future & Temporal Oddities

Alternative Calendars Used in Isolated Communities

In certain remote areas, time isn't measured by the Gregorian calendar. Instead, communities sync their clocks with crop cycles, hunting seasons, or spiritual traditions. Some villages begin their year with the first snowfall, others shape months according to lunar phases or animal migrations. On Pacific islands, months are tied to the tides, while in some mountainous regions, the year starts when certain flowers bloom. These alternative systems show that concepts like "month" or "year" aren't fixed—they reflect local rhythms and natural cues, blending timekeeping with the land's heartbeat and demonstrating how culture molds our perception of time.

Prophets Who Foresaw Modern Inventions

Throughout history, a few visionaries seemed to predict future technologies. Leonardo da Vinci's sketches of flying machines hinted at helicopters centuries before their invention. Jules Verne imagined electric submarines and space travel when they were pure fantasy. In the 19th century, journalists and writers speculated about "horseless carriages" long before the automobile's rise. One researcher found that many past authors envisioned concepts mirroring today's tech, proving that human imagination often plants the seeds of tomorrow's reality long before it emerges.

Ancient Literature's Idea of Time Travel

Long before modern sci-fi, ancient texts toyed with journeys through time. Some Hindu legends describe heroes who sleep for centuries and awaken to a changed world. In Chinese tales, a traveler enters a cave and reappears decades later. A comparative literature expert notes that even in Hellenistic times there were stories about characters "out of sync" with their era. Such narratives prove our longing to break time's linear flow is as old as storytelling itself—an ancient dream of escaping the "here and now."

The Internet Era Imagined a Century Ago

In the early 1900s, some European futurists and American pioneers envisioned global communication networks. Newspapers mentioned "tele-newspapers" and distant knowledge archives, conceptual ancestors of the Internet. In 1890, a French novelist described a "mechanical brain" accessible to everyone. A tech historian found at least 20 authors from 1850 to 1920 who dreamed up similar systems. These visions show that human creativity often precedes actual invention, sowing ideas that flourish decades later.

Old Clocks That Measured More Than Just Time

Ancient civilizations didn't rely solely on hourglasses. Water clocks (clepsydras), incense clocks, and candle clocks were used not just to measure hours but to guide rituals and daily tasks. In some Asian temples, lines on burning incense sticks marked intervals for meditation sessions. A cultural ethnologist notes these methods show time wasn't just about counting hours, but integrating human activity with elements like fire, water, scent, and ceremony.

Bizarre Time Zones in Small Nations

Not all countries follow neat hourly offsets. Nepal sets its clock 45 minutes off GMT, and parts of Australia operate on half-hour increments. Such choices, often political or historical, can mean stepping across a border changes the time by 30 minutes. A geographer explains these quirks reflect local interests—aligning daylight better or asserting cultural identity. Time thus becomes a cultural and political compromise, not just lines on a globe.

The Phenomenon of the 'Delayed' New Year

Not everywhere does the new year begin on January 1. In Ethiopia, the new year starts in September; in Iran, Nowruz matches the spring equinox. The adoption of the Gregorian calendar over the Julian one occurred at different times, causing confusion. Russia switched in 1918, "skipping" several days. A historian recounts how some regions ended up celebrating two new years in a row. These delays and differences remind us that time isn't absolute—it's fluid, shaped by history and politics.

Time in Parallel Dimensions:

Some imagine parallel universes where history took different turns: what if Napoleon won at Waterloo, or Rome never fell? Such speculative ideas populate novels, comics, and online forums. A sociologist found that 40% of sci-fi fans love discussing alternate timelines. Though no evidence supports multiple timelines, the concept lets us escape linear reality. It's human nature to dream of "other" times where history diverges, even if they remain mental playgrounds rather than proven truths.

Past Predictions of Futures That Never Came True

In past centuries, "futurologists" predicted scenarios that never materialized: personal flying cars by 2000, underwater cities, holidays on Mars. A review of old newspapers shows that over 70% of long-term forecasts missed the mark. Instead of accuracy, they offered hope and creativity. Even if incorrect, these predictions inspire and provoke thought. They remind us that tomorrow's landscape is uncertain, and human imagination often outpaces reality.

Time Machines in Secret (or Nearly So) Museums

Some eccentric museums display "time machines" allegedly built by quirky inventors. None actually work, but they enchant visitors seeking wonder. A reporter describes an exhibition featuring a 19th-century contraption claiming temporal travels—actually a futurist sculpture. These displays are more art than science, symbols of our fascination with transcending time's barriers. No proof, but much delight in imagining someone tried the impossible.

Alternate Timelines in Comics

Pop culture loves alternate timelines: heroes meeting their younger selves, universes where villains triumph and heroes fail. Marvel and DC Comics exploit these twists to keep stories fresh. A comics historian says these narrative tricks let creators "reboot" characters, ask "what if?" and keep readers hooked. It's a creative move that treats time as malleable clay, allowing infinite story variations and renewing familiar worlds endlessly.

Archeology of the Future: Imagining Tomorrow's Past

A speculative discipline ponders how future beings might interpret our present millennia from now. Some futurists imagine robot-archaeologists decoding our smartphones as tribal amulets. Today we excavate ancient ruins; tomorrow, someone might dig through our digital debris. It inverts roles: instead of us studying the past, future historians will study us as distant relics. This game of perspective shows that time's arrow can reverse, making us artifacts in an unknown era's museum.

Endless Nights Near the Earth's Poles

Near the poles, extended daylight or darkness distorts our sense of day and night. In summer, the sun never sets; in winter, it barely rises. Locals rely on clocks more than sunlight. A Norwegian researcher notes that in Svalbard, 60% of residents find "day" and "night" lose their meaning. These conditions prove that humans don't dictate time's rhythm; the planet's tilt and orbit do, challenging our standard notions of daily cycles.

Atomic Clocks and Incredible Precision

Today, we measure time with atomic clocks so precise they lose a second every millions of years—an accuracy unimaginable to our ancestors. These clocks power GPS, telecommunications, and scientific experiments. A physicist points out that without atomic precision, modern technology would crumble. This represents a radical shift from ancient methods where an hour could be off by minutes. Now a tiny temporal error can disrupt entire systems, a testament to how far we've come in mastering time.

The 10-Day Week

During the French Revolution, they tried a decimal week of 10 days instead of 7—a radical attempt to align time with revolutionary ideals. It failed because it clashed with ingrained habits. Similar reforms elsewhere also fizzled. A sociologist notes that altering shared temporal structures is tough: time is a social contract forged over centuries. These trials reveal how deeply time is woven into culture, making radical changes a challenge.

The Man Who Tried to Stop Time

Some artists or performers attempted symbolic gestures to "stop" time—standing motionless for hours or halting a town's clocks. A Japanese performer once remained immobile for 24 hours in a busy station, a poetic protest against modern frenzy. Such acts aren't scientific feats, but metaphors: we can't truly halt time, but we can make people think about its relentless flow. They show our longing to control the uncontrollable, to slow down a river that never stops.

Aztec Prophecies That Never Happened

Aztec and Maya calendars described cosmic cycles, sometimes misinterpreted as doomsday predictions by our modern minds. The Maya didn't foresee world's end in 2012, just the close of a cycle. An anthropologist notes that many ancient "prophecies" were symbolic, not literal. We learn caution: not every old prediction is catastrophic or final. Often they were conceptual frameworks for understanding the cosmos, rather than literal countdowns to disaster.

Time Zones Invented for Political Reasons

Some countries tweak official time for political or economic motives—half-hour offsets, year-round daylight savings, or even aligning themselves differently from former colonial powers. This can yield quirky situations. A political analyst sees these decisions as tools of national identity. Official time, thus, isn't just a natural fact but can be shaped by human agendas. The clock on your wall may reflect geopolitics as much as geography.

Animal Perceptions of Time

Studies suggest some animals experience time differently. A fly's rapid image processing makes a second feel longer; an elephant's slower heart rate might render an hour more relaxed. An ethologist notes that physiology shapes the sense of duration. This challenges our idea of "seconds" and "minutes" as universal units. What's a blink to us might be a drawn-out moment to an insect. Time, it seems, can stretch or shrink depending on who's watching.

Interstellar Travel and Time Dilation

Einstein's relativity shows that near light-speed travel time "flows" differently. An astronaut speeding through space ages more slowly than someone on Earth. Sci-fi embraces these paradoxes, envisioning civilizations fractured by differing time scales. A physicist says if one day we attempt to colonize distant star systems, these effects become practical reality. Thus, time evolves from a daily concept into an elastic dimension, opening doors to cosmic exploration and philosophical debate about the essence of time.

Chapter 20:
The Great Mixture—Random Revelations

Coincidences Too Strange to Be Mere Chance

Some stories seem to defy logic: a person surviving multiple shipwrecks, a novel that predicted a real-life disaster years in advance, letters hinting at future events that later actually occurred. A researcher cataloged hundreds of "extreme coincidences," enough to rattle even the most skeptical minds. Chance or destiny? Statisticians say it's just probability: out of billions of events, some align in eerie ways. Yet when it happens, witnesses feel a chill. It's as if the world winks at us, reminding us reality sometimes seems to flirt with fate, teasing us with patterns we can't fully explain.

Weird Collections from Every Corner of the World

Some collect only blue pen caps, others hoard thousands of chipped teacups or broken pencils. A Belgian collector owns over 5,000 different bar napkins. An American proudly shows off the largest assortment of mismatched slippers. These bizarre gatherings, often incomprehensible to outsiders, hold emotional or symbolic value for their owners. They prove that any object, however mundane, can become treasure to someone. It's a testament to human imagination and passion for the unusual—where even a pen cap can become a priceless artifact.

Letters Delivered Decades Late

Imagine a letter mailed in 1950 but arriving in 2000, after wandering through postal depots, forgotten bags, and shuttered offices. A mundane note turns into a message from the past, charged with nostalgia. Postal archives record hundreds of such cases. A routine correspondence transforms into a time capsule bridging epochs. Each envelope can become an accidental time machine, granting the recipient the thrill of discovering thoughts and news from a long-lost era.

Elevators That Move Diagonally

Who says elevators must only go straight up and down? Experimental prototypes in Germany and Japan allow oblique movements, challenging the standard "floor-to-floor" concept. Imagine traveling between buildings without stepping outside, gliding diagonally like an indoor cable car. Early 2000s trials never took off commercially, but they show how innovation can subvert habits, hinting that verticality need not be absolute. Even a common infrastructure like an elevator can be reinvented when creativity takes the lead.

People Living on Islands of Plastic Waste

In the Pacific, massive "garbage patches" of plastic float on the ocean's surface. Some activists and artists tried consolidating this debris into habitable platforms—artificial "plastic islands" serving as labs or temporary shelters. Although marginal ideas so far, they reveal a desperate creativity when facing environmental crises. Living on a plastic island sounds insane, yet it symbolizes humanity's strained relationship with pollution. It's a metaphor of our era: transforming trash into a habitat, a startling pivot from disaster to resource, if only in experimental form.

World Records for the Longest Hair

Some individuals never cut their hair, reaching astonishing lengths. A Chinese woman once flaunted a five-meter-long mane; an Indian man grew a beard over two meters. These Guinness feats embody extreme patience and dedication. A 2020 report suggests around 200 people worldwide maintain such lengths for cultural, spiritual, or personal reasons. Whether symbols of identity or self-challenge, these hair records remind us that even not cutting one's hair can become an epic journey, turning an everyday act into a lifelong adventure.

Villages Where Everyone Shares the Same Surname

In isolated communities, centuries of intermarriage led to nearly everyone sharing the same last name. In a certain Italian hamlet, hundreds bear identical surnames, causing headaches for registration offices and mail carriers. The streets teem with near-homonyms, forcing residents to invent nicknames to distinguish neighbors. An ethnographer notes that such phenomena reflect geographical isolation and stable social structures. It's a curious anomaly—like a village frozen in time—where identity blurs into one large extended family.

Contests for the World's Strangest Mustaches

There are international competitions dedicated to mustaches and beards sculpted into absurd forms: meticulously twisted curls, spiral moustaches, facial hair shaped into geometric patterns. In Germany, mustache artistry championships draw hundreds of contestants. A French participant once molded his mustache into an Eiffel Tower shape, earning applause and bafflement. It's folklore and creativity rolled into one, transforming facial hair into living sculptures. Proof that the human body can serve as a canvas, and a simple moustache can become a whimsical show and a proud competition.

Ghost Photos

Since photography's invention, some images have been hailed as evidence of ghosts. But many were later explained as reflections, double exposures, or clever tricks. A photography historian notes that in the 1800s there was a craze for "spectral" photos, with people delighting in deceiving the gullible. Today, despite advanced tech, we still yearn to believe in the supernatural. Pictures of "phantoms" remain a play between eye, mind, and the desire for wonder—proof that we often see what we want to see, more than what's actually there.

Sculptures Made from Chewed Gum

Some artists create installations out of used chewing gum, molding them like sticky clay. Disgusting? Perhaps. But there's a "Gum Wall" in Seattle, covered in thousands of colorful wads, now a tourist attraction. Turning squishy waste into art is a bold, if odd, statement. It reminds us that creativity can sprout anywhere, even from saliva-laden refuse, challenging notions of beauty and worth. The sticky gum becomes ephemeral artwork, flipping the concept of trash upside down.

Square Coins and Plastic Banknotes

Not all currencies follow standard shapes. Some countries have issued square coins; others print banknotes on polymer instead of paper. The Cook Islands introduced triangular coins; Canada uses transparent polymer bills. An economist notes that monetary value lies in social convention, not in material form. These experiments show money's malleability—both literally and figuratively. Currency can reflect national identity or technical needs, proving that finance can embrace innovation and defy expectations.

Musical Roads That Sing as You Drive

In parts of Japan and California, special grooves in the pavement produce musical notes when tires roll over them. Your car becomes a needle on a giant vinyl record, turning a drive into a melody. An engineer explains that pitch changes with driving speed, transforming a mundane journey into a serenade of asphalt. This surprise combo of transportation and tune reminds us that infrastructure can delight as well as serve. Driving becomes a performance, a duet between rubber and road.

Artist Colonies Living Underground

Some artist communities dwell in caves or old mines, shaping dark, cramped spaces into homes, studios, and galleries. In Australia's Coober Pedy, people live below ground to escape heat, while some creatives find inspiration underground. An anthropologist describes these settlements as tiny utopias, where art and isolation meet. Subterranean life flips our idea of home and studio, proving creativity can bloom even in the Earth's depths, defying the need for sunlight and open horizons.

Giant Pinhole Cameras

Some photographers turn entire rooms into pinhole cameras: a tiny hole on one wall projects the outside scene inside, reversed. A Mexican artist once transformed a bedroom into a camera obscura, capturing a huge image on the opposite wall. In the digital age, this primitive setup feels magical, recalling photography's essence—just light and a hole. It's a timeless optical trick that ignores technology's complexity, making photography a spatial experience rather than a mere click.

Bridges Made from Living Roots

In the rainforests of Northeast India, tribes guide tree roots across streams until they form natural bridges. Over decades, these living structures strengthen rather than weaken. A biologist found some of these root bridges hundreds of years old. This is organic architecture at its finest: humans gently steer nature's growth to build infrastructure. Crossing a root bridge feels like walking inside nature's handshake—a quiet, green marvel blending botany and engineering, proving that patience can create wonders more durable than stone or steel.

Cryptocurrencies Born from Strange Memes

In the digital era, money can emerge from jokes. Cryptocurrencies like Dogecoin, inspired by a dog meme, soared in popularity despite starting as a prank. Others feature cats, bananas, or aliens. A financial analyst admits these "meme-coins" attracted real investors, showing that value can emerge from online humor. Money becomes parody, a reflection of our chaotic age where economy and internet culture collide, blurring the line between serious finance and playful irony.

Houses Inside Abandoned Buses

Some repurpose old, discarded buses as tiny homes or mobile studios. Students, hippies, and artists refurbish these shells into cozy abodes on wheels. A Canadian woman turned a school bus into a loft, complete with kitchenette and bed. It's recycling at its finest—turning a vehicle destined for scrap into a living space. Nomadic design meets sustainability, proving that where others see junk, creative minds see potential for freedom and travel.

Penguin Colonies in Unexpected Places

We picture penguins on icy shores, but some colonies thrive in milder climates—South African coasts, for instance, host tuxedoed birds adapting to warmer shores. It shatters the polar stereotype. An ornithologist notes that certain penguin species flourish in surprising habitats, showing nature's flexibility. These birds become ambassadors of adaptability, reminding us not to box creatures into fixed images. Penguins can prosper beyond the snowy horizon we imagine.

Underground Metropolises and Invisible Cities

Beneath our feet lie entire worlds: Roman catacombs, smuggling tunnels, modern underground malls. Derinkuyu in Cappadocia sheltered thousands below ground. Tokyo's subterranean passages form hidden commercial networks. An urban planner calls these invisible layers a "second planet" underneath us. It's a reminder that cities have more dimensions than we perceive. The world expands downward, harboring secret lives and tunnels, reconfiguring our notion of urban space.

People Spending Life in Hot-Air Balloons

Finally, consider those who choose to live in balloons or airships, drifting with the winds. Historically, adventurers tried spending months aloft—cooking, sleeping, and existing above the clouds. A French explorer in the 1800s attempted a round-the-world balloon voyage, failing but leaving an unforgettable idea: life on the breeze, far from earthly constraints. It's a soaring ode to freedom, challenging every convention and whispering: "Why not?" in the face of gravity and routine.

Thanks for Making It This Far

You've journeyed through a long series of oddities, surprises, and unusual glimpses into the world. Maybe you stumbled upon a fact that genuinely struck a chord, or discovered a bit of trivia you'd love to share with a friend. If you feel like letting me know how this reading experience has been for you—what intrigued you the most, what made you smile or think—just remember that your opinion will be valuable to those who pick up these pages in the future. Every comment, whether enthusiastic or more critical, can help me understand what works and what can be improved. I'll personally read your thoughts, taking them as a helpful guide for the readers who will come after you.

Scan to leave a review on Amazon if you live in the US

Scan to leave a review on Amazon if you live in the UK

Scan to leave a review on Amazon if you live in Canada

Scan to leave a review on Amazon if you live in Australia

Conclusion

Here we are at the end of this journey through curiosities and oddities, a map-free itinerary that led you to unexpected places—creatures adapting to impossible conditions, out-of-the-ordinary calendars, bizarre records, and collections of objects you'd never have deemed valuable. As you turned the pages, you encountered penguins thriving far from icy shores, letters delivered decades late, alternative timelines, diagonal elevators, room-sized pinhole cameras, floating trash islands repurposed as habitats, and even living root bridges. It felt like strolling through a bazaar of the unusual, where every stall offered its own little hidden treasure.

Perhaps during your reading, you experienced that pleasant sense of bewilderment—like when you gaze at something peculiar and think, "I never imagined this could exist." That was precisely the goal: showing you how many shades of strangeness and wonder dwell in our world, often concealed beneath the surface of the everyday. Maybe you chuckled at sculpted mustaches, pondered over oddly shaped coins, or imagined life in a village full of near-identical surnames. Or you may have pictured yourself building a home in an old bus. Even if none of these tidbits serve you directly, each adds a piece to the puzzle of understanding our planet's complexity, human creativity, and nature's infinite adaptability.

There's no ultimate meaning to extract from this mosaic of facts: the beauty lies precisely in the absence of a rigid theme. Reality isn't a novel with a neat storyline—it's a vast catalog of surprises. You've seen how each chapter, each curiosity, tells its own story, yet fits together into a picture of endless variety. This book, designed to accompany your quietest, most private moments, aimed to show that nothing is as ordinary as it seems. Behind appearances lie stories, inventions, customs, and absurdities that expand the horizons of your mind.

Perhaps from now on you'll see familiar objects in a new light, or recall a peculiar anecdote to amaze your friends. Maybe you'll start spotting extraordinary potential in everyday life, because if there's one lesson in this "great mixture," it's that the world is rich with facets, details, and ideas that challenge our certainties. Next time you settle onto your "throne" at home, even without the book in hand, your mind might wander back through what you've read—floating plastic islands, puzzling ancient clocks, subterranean cities.

The adventure extends beyond these pages: the hints you've encountered here are just a taste of countless stories awaiting anyone curious enough to seek them out. Once you close the book, you can transform every "empty" moment into a chance to uncover new marvels. The universe of curiosities is inexhaustible, always ready to offer fresh revelations at random. Now it's your turn: stay alert, open-minded, ready to be surprised. The world is a giant container of secrets, and you hold the key to discovering them. Enjoy what lies ahead.

About the Author

If you're picturing a solemn scholar locked away in a dusty library, Sam Callister isn't your guy. He's the kind of person who never stopped asking "Why?" about every odd thing in the world. While classmates collected trading cards, Sam collected bizarre anecdotes, nature's strangest phenomena, quirky cultural traditions, and random absurd facts scattered across the globe.

You might find him jotting notes in a worn-out notebook, recording details about an obscure village festival or a square coin spotted in a barely-known museum. He's the sort who'd happily spend a whole day rummaging through attics, back rooms, and archives, just to uncover forgotten treasures. Not to pen an academic treatise, but simply to say, "Hey, did you know...?"

In everyday life, Sam doesn't sport eccentric hats or sculpt his mustache into giraffe shapes (at least not yet), but he's always the first to be thrilled when he stumbles on a new curiosity. For him, the world is a giant jigsaw of oddities assembled at random, without needing any rigid logic—just the sheer delight of surprising himself and others.

If you're reading this book, chances are Sam Callister has succeeded: he's invited you into his warehouse of wonders, swinging open the doors to both the absurd and the marvelous. Don't expect absolute truths, but rather a collection of astonishing flashes of insight, gathered by someone unafraid to say, "I'll never stop being amazed!" That's Sam: someone who's learned that knowledge doesn't require a classroom—just a whole lot of curiosity.

Printed in Great Britain
by Amazon